PENTEC
CHARISMATIC
WOMEN

CONSTRUCTIONS OF FEMININITY IN ALEXANDRA TOWNSHIP

TUMI MAMPANE

HSRC
PRESS

Published by HSRC Press
Private Bag X9182, Cape Town, 8000, South Africa
www.hsrcpress.ac.za

First published 2023

ISBN (soft cover) 978-0-7969-2639-5
ISBN (PDF)

This book has undergone a double-blind independent peer-review process overseen by the HSRC Press Editorial Board.

The views expressed in this publication are those of the authors. They do not necessarily reflect the views or policies of the Human Sciences Research Council (the Council) or indicate that the Council endorses the views of the authors. In quoting from this publication, readers are advised to attribute the source of the information to the individual author concerned and not to the Council.

The publishers have no responsibility for the continued existence or accuracy of URLs for external or third-party Internet websites referred to in this book and do not guarantee that any content on such websites is, or will remain, accurate or appropriate.

Copy edited by Karen Press
Typeset by Richard Jones
Cover design by Nic Jooste
Printed by Capitil Press, Cape Town, South Africa

Distributed in Africa by Blue Weaver
Tel: +27 (021) 701 4477; Fax Local: (021) 701 7302; Fax International: 0927865242139
www.blueweaver.co.za

Distributed in Europe and the United Kingdom by Eurospan Distribution Services (EDS)
Tel: +44 (0) 17 6760 4972; Fax: +44 (0) 17 6760 1640
www.eurospanbookstore.com

Distributed in the US, its possessions, Canada, and Asia by Lynne Rienner Publishers, Inc.
Tel: +1 303-444-6684; Fax: +1 303-444-0824; Email: cservice@rienner.com
www.rienner.com

To copy any part of this publication, you may contact DALRO for information and copyright clearance.
Tel: 010 822 7469 (from within South Africa); +27 (0)10 822 7469
Fax: +27 (86) 648 1136
Email: dalro@dalro.co.za
Postal Address: PostNet Suite #018, PO Box 9951, Sandton, 2146, South Africa
www.dalro.co.za

Any unauthorised copying could lead to civil liability and/or criminal sanctions.
Suggested citation: Tumi Mampane (2023) *Pentecostal Charismatic Women: Constructions of Femininity in Alexandra Township*. Cape Town: HSRC Press

Contents

List of figures   v
Acronyms and abbreviations   vi
Note on translations   vii
Acknowledgements   viii
Dedication   x
Preface   xi

Chapter 1   Becoming Charismatic women   **1**
Pentecostal history: Identity re/formations   3
Black feminist theology   6
Womanism, Black feminism and African feminism   7
Entry points   9

Chapter 2   Contested Pentecostalisms: A review   **12**
Have you read the Comaroffs?   12
Upward mobility, breaking from the past and the prosperity
gospel   14
Mediated Pentecostalism and shaping 'the world'   18
Gendered ideologies and identities   21
A problematic view   27
Conclusion   29

**Chapter 3   Between the feminised other and Black
women's power**   **30**
Beyond the feminised other   30
African gender discourses: Religion, culture and the law   32
Gender as performativity   40
Wilful whispers   42
Conclusion   43

Chapter 4   This field I call home   **45**

Chapter 5   Constructions of femininity   **61**
Get me to the church on time   61
When church is in session   67

Living Waters Ministries   68
Upper Hall Ministries   69
God's Love Ministries   69
Red Sea Ministries   70
The sermons   71
Pastor Mabaso's poem   71
The sound of wedding bells   73
Same bells, different ideologies   76
Women in the pulpit   78
Men in the pulpit   81
From the mouths of babes – *Bomthandazo*   84
Desire: Marriage, heterosexual love   85
Going 50/50: Definitions of equality and gender roles   88
Prayer scarves: Respectability and the female fear factory   94
We don't want to be judged   102
Pastor fuckboys and the art of dating   105
Femininity from their mothers to their churches   108
What's love got to do with it?   109
Conclusion   112

Chapter 6   A question of difference   **115**

About the author   119
Photo gallery   120
Notes   125
References   127
Index   139

List of figures

Figure 1.1. Nkuli Silawuli, worship leader. 11

Figure 4.1. Easter lunch set-up, 2019, hosted by Red Sea Ministries at Thusong Youth Centre. 60

Figure 4.2. 'At home' with my mother, singing at a special service. 60

Figure P1. Bishop Silawuli and Pastor Thoko (my mother). 120

Figure P2. Pastor Patrick and his wife Mrs Sexoka, Nkuli in the background. 120

Figure P3. Nkuli leading worship at Thusong Youth Centre. 121

Figure P4. Phutaditjaba Community Centre and a young, unnamed beneficiary. 122

Figure P5. Ko Bareng (The Bar). 122

Figure P6. Ko Bareng patrons (left–right): Mahlangu, John Namane and John Masangu. 123

Figure P7. One of Alexandra's oldest homes. 123

Figure P8. Another 'old home' in Alexandra, protected by a wall. 124

Figure P9. 15th Avenue on Hofmeyr Street, Alexandra. 124

Figure P10. The Roosevelt Street entrance to Pan Africa, Alexandra. 125

Acronyms and abbreviations

BCom	bachelor of commerce
GPS	Global Positioning System
MC	master of ceremonies
LGBTQI+	lesbian, gay, bisexual, transgender, queer or intersex
MMC	Mighty Men's Conference
PhD	doctor of philosophy
PK	Pastors' Kids
SLIM	Single Ladies Interdenominational Ministry
Unisa	University of South Africa
ZAOGA	Zimbabwe Assemblies of God Africa

Note on translations

All translations are my own. The use of prefixes for words in African languages is reserved only for the original narratives. For instance, in the original the Zulu language is *isiZulu* and the people are named *amaZulu*, but in English I refer to them as Zulu speakers and to the language as Zulu. This is based on the translation of other languages into English. I use several South Africanisms in my text and only translate some of them. Explanations of the others can be found in the *South African Oxford Dictionary* (Dictionary Unit for South African English 2011).

My research participants are from differing backgrounds and use different languages to communicate. Those who come from the former 'homelands' are more likely to speak fluently in their languages, but most of those who are either native to Alexandra (as I am) or have lived in the township for a long time tend to speak a mixture of languages. Typical sentences in Alexandra mix Zulu, Tswana, Sotho and occasionally Xhosa, Pedi and Afrikaans. Most sermons are delivered in English with a mixture of African languages to cater for speakers of all languages. For this reason, except where the original is entirely in English, I place the original words of the participants quoted in the text in italics, followed by the translation into standard English in square brackets.

Acknowledgements

Pier Paolo,
You missed an opportunity to puff out your chest and tease, 'tell me I was right – again!' Or maybe you are missing nothing, because I hear your Italian accent clearly when your crazy predictions and dreams for me come to fruition. I am writing this letter to let you know, once again and probably not for the last time, that you were in fact right. You were always right.

You were right about my finally meeting and working closely with Pumla Dineo Gqola. You said that I would find my African feminist 'comrades' (your favourite word) and that Pumla would be the best inspiration I never had. Pumla is our dream come true.

You were right to push me to contact Aphiwe Ntlhemeza, another African feminist whose love and support I can always rely upon.

You said that there are a lot of people rooting for me besides you and my immediate family. I thank Constance Kasiyamhuru, Thandeka Bukula, Mbongeni Msimanga, Sifiso Mnisi, Linda Zwane and many others in my different networks for proving you, once again, right!

A lot of work went into the writing and thinking through of this book. A lot of it was done at restaurants where you would foot the bill, and a lot more was done in the safety of your study. You honed a space for me, so generously, always generously, to work and to think and to drink too much coffee; and you always made sure that each cup was followed by a glass of refreshing water. I worked while talking through gnawing ideas with you. I watched your face keenly for expressions that either agreed with what I was saying or asked for more. Some of this work was done in tears when you would hold me during a late-night call. And more as we danced to kwaito, reggae and African jazz.

I listen to our recorded conversations even as I write this letter, to remind myself (though I need no prompts to remember you, PP) of your affirming voice and of your sharp intellect and of your gentle yet stern reminders that I must eat and of the world of knowledge that you opened to me and of your questions. Your questions. Your quest to make me see myself as a writer. I sit with questions; I sit with your questions. I sit and I live, and I teach and write, and I mother a cool and amazing girl, always with your quest firmly in my support. The family of which you became an honorary member, Tebza, Dimzo, Bubu, DJ Barz, Nqonqo, Bontle and Tish, holds me in ways I can never be grateful enough for. Our family believes in Your quest.

You were gentle and kind in just the right ways. You had a quest for yourself, too: to listen more than you speak. I wish I had found better ways to tell you that You listen so intently and with more heart than most people I know. It was your ear – Your Heart – that gave me just enough courage to see this project through. My luck may be that hearts – Your Heart, PP – live forever.

You may hate this letter, and You may shout, 'no, no, no, no, NO! How can I take credit for work that you did by yourself, Tumi Mampane: you!' But we both know how these conversations end: with me laughing at your modesty and finding creative ways to credit you anyways.

This book is for Us, PP. It is the beginning of all the wonders you dreamt up for me. It is my wonderful reminder of your face, your voice, your kind eyes and your delicious food. It is my reminder of all that I have and all that I lost when I lost You.

But you will tell me not to think of you as a loss. You will tell me to take this moment in and celebrate it with a glass of wine. I do not want you to be right – not this time – but you are. I will drink, laugh, write and share glorious moments with friends, students, colleagues and family. And I will raise every glass in honour of You.

Thank You always for being right,
Tumi

PS. I know that this letter is Small. The Big Things lurk inside. The Big Things are in the air and the trees that You inhabit so rightly.

Dedication

Always for My Tish who dances, and sings,
and laughs with a world of energy beneath her blessed feet.

Preface

How to liberate my true hope? Everything is against me.
The first obstacle to my escape is this woman's body barring my way,
a voluptuous body with closed eyes, voluntarily blind,
stretched out full, ready to perish.
– Simone de Beauvoir, *The second sex* (2010: 14–15)

I am a member of a Pentecostal church. I grew up in church, first as a Methodist, but I was still very young when my parents converted to Pentecostalism. I am using this word with reservation, and as a person alienated from it. When I grew up, we did not identify as 'Pentecostal' or 'Charismatic' but rather as *abazalwane*, which means born again. So, in this book, I use the terms interchangeably to speak both to the scholarly literature and to the lived registers of my community. The shifts between registers of knowledge, knowing and living locate me in differing ways. I write as an academic, as a woman who grew up in Alexandra township, and as a woman who as a girl worshipped a male god.

As time went by and I was growing up, some things were gnawing at me. They still are, especially the messages that are given in church and how or whether I fit into these messages as a woman. So, I started this project to see if there are other women who, like me, are having their pastors' sermons gnaw at them, and whether and how they are handling this. Do they take it all as the absolute truth, the Word of God? Or are they negotiating these teachings? Do Pentecostal women apply their pastors' sermons in their lives with friends, colleagues, families and partners?

When I started my research, I initially pushed myself into a corner. The question I asked was: are women in Pentecostal churches oppressed or liberated? But I soon realised that if the questions I ask are based only on oppression versus liberation, and I can only answer them in terms of how power structures define and constrain agency, then there is nothing in between, and no other way of thinking and being. I will get stuck. But more than that, I thought, I will fall into the same line of thinking that I oppose throughout this book: one that does not investigate and see Black women as subjects with an interior life; one that ignores the complexities and intersections of being a Black woman.

This is why I begin my introduction in Chapter 1 by presenting femininity as a construction that comes from the outside, but also as a set of constructions that we recreate within us: constructions of being a woman, becoming a woman for oneself and becoming one for others. I outline the key concepts that frame the discussion of African Pentecostalism and its constructions of femininity throughout the book. I also outline how my study intervenes in broader African and global feminist debates about femininity and 'becoming women'. I focus on the interventions made by African and diasporic feminisms in theorising this becoming. This book also challenges the rigid assumptions of many Pentecostal scholars about feminine identities, and their explanations of what attracts African women to the Pentecostal movement.

In discussing oppression, I am guided by Sara Ahmed's view of oppression as 'pressure' that does not always need force and sometimes takes 'happy' forms (Ahmed 2017). I am not 'unhappy', and neither are the women I speak to and whose lives I foreground in this book. Yet, we are not 'happy', even as we clap, dance and sing in church – our designated happy place. Ahmed places us, women who are from a different setting to hers, quite accurately: as figures of a pressure for happiness in the form of a life with which we do not necessarily want to identify.

I attended an overwhelmingly white Anglican school for girls that identified as feminist. We were always encouraged to read feminist texts and question the representations of women in the media and literature. So, I have always been questioning happiness, but I also learned early on to question the 'pressures' that I experienced to pursue happiness as an embodiment of whiteness and a rejection of my Blackness. Constantly, the feminists at school found different ways to show the young woman I was becoming that I would be so much happier if I could be whiter. This is another happy place that I rejected. So, over the years, I have sought out women who could speak more directly to my experiences and contexts: women who know the life of resisting whiteness and the temptations of its proximities, heteronormativity and male gods. What we have in common is that we know the effects of patriarchy, sexism, racism and heterosexism, and we want to find a way out. We write ourselves out. That is the common cause that I find in the feminist strands that I call Blackwomen scholarship.

This book draws on Blackwomen theory to highlight distinct yet shared Black and African feminist articulations in an attempt not only to add to the growing body of work on Charismatic African Pentecostal communities and practices, but also to contest the fetishising and othering tendencies of white anthropologists who claim to conduct similar studies. A part of me sympathises with this anthropological take on Pentecostal studies by my counterparts: many of them are taught to walk into uncharted territory and look for the 'savage slot'. And in order to sell this savage, one must sensationalise her. In this book, I talk of how anthropologists have sensationalised Black women in Pentecostal churches, and reduced them to upwardly mobile professionals who are fitted into categories such as Romany Creams and Oreos, when they are not being described as deranged or hopelessly oppressed. The very spaces in which anthropologists exist give them that savage slot, and without it they may feel that they cannot produce a good piece of academic writing.

As both a lifelong resident of Alexandra township and a practising member of the Charismatic Pentecostal tradition, I utilise my 'outsider within' status as a Black woman (auto) ethnographer to bring out the stories about us and sides of us that are overlooked by current scholarship. I use my position as a 'native' to destabilise the savage slot, to show that it does not have to exist, that there does not have to be this great sensationalism. We can talk about Black women just living their lives and realise that in this simplicity lies a complexity of interiority. This book reveals the ways in which the Charismatic women of Alexandra build strong bonds with one another despite their differences, and contest controlling images of femininity even as they sometimes traffic in problematic heteronormative constructions of social life.

I examine Charismatic discourses that build the gender identities of women congregants. I also observe how women churchgoers come to an understanding of their desires and ideas about respectability and shame, and record their interactions and negotiations with the discourses of their churches. This book gives insights into Alexandra Pentecostal women's personal perceptions, embodiments and performances of the self within the church and in the wider societal spaces that women churchgoers occupy. It does not merely apply feminist concepts and theories, but demonstrates how the subject of femininity in African Charismatic Pentecostal churches is multidimensional, contested and not without contradiction.

The words in the epigraph to this preface, in which Simone de Beauvoir quotes her friend, Colette to show the importance and constraining qualities of the gendered body, ring hauntingly for me, as I am sure they do for other women. I am equally haunted by words such as those of a caller on PowerFM who said this to me during an interview about my research: 'It is unfortunate... But this is how God has created the world to be. Women must submit to men. God has given men the power. That is just how things are'. I agree: it is unfortunate. It is unfortunate that we, as a society, close each other out of important conversations that could liberate us all, because we want so desperately to hold on to the image of an all-empowering, masculine, white and violent god.

It is my hope that this book will intervene in scholarship on religion, spirituality, community and gender to keep these conversations open and interlinked. The text should be read as my account as a knower of the world, as well as a negotiation of how others know the world. I wrote this book to both question and assert knowledge, and each chapter brings its own set of questions even as it firmly holds to the voices of my participants. If you are to be haunted or moved, you should pay close attention to the words of the Pentecostal Charismatic women of Alexandra township transcribed in this text.

Chapter 1

Becoming Charismatic women

I also want to get to that point when I'm able to balance my love for going out and having a good time with my love for church. I want to be able to do everything I love without people judging me. So, I'm working on it slowly because I also don't want to make people feel uncomfortable.

— Ntsiki, 24-year-old IT intern

Growing up in a Christian home, I witnessed three different parenting approaches taken by my mother and father, where my sisters and I were concerned. When my one sister came into teenagehood, she started to show an interest in boys, and it was well reciprocated. My mother described the boys as bees following honey. It was decided by my parents then that a drastic haircut would do well to, if not stop this dangerous attraction altogether, at least minimise it. That was the end of my sister's gorgeous dark mane until she grew it back years later as an adult. My other sister, shy and reserved, shaved her head out of choice. She no longer wished to deal with the high maintenance of good hair – a decision I thought would be a relief to my parents. Yet, to all of our surprise, they were unhappy with her action to put the 'bees' off, and instead worried that her 'boyish' look and behaviour would mean that she would stay single forever. Constant talk and not so subtle hints about femininity and a feminine look went on in our home for months, until my sister finally gave in and grew her hair back into dreadlocks. I, on the other hand, had no choices when it came to my hair as it simply did not grow. Every kind of nourishing, treating, fast-growth hair product was bought to help me look prettier, and none of them worked. My hair stayed 'boyish' and, as a remedy of sorts, to this day I only own a few pairs of pants. Simone de Beauvoir says, 'one is not born, but rather becomes, a woman' (2010: 14). My sisters and I are perfect examples of this.

I begin this chapter with an epigraph and a personal anecdote as reflections on becoming. This becoming does not happen in a homogeneous manner for all girls, even girls growing up in the same home. But more than this, becoming is a process of socialisation that involves a self who is outside of the self and for others (Butler 2004). The first of the sisters I describe became through attraction to boys, and became also through an intervention – though maybe 'intrusion' is a better word – from our parents. The same was true for my other sister, who became what was recognised as more feminine. Our socialisation into recognition, then, became for us, for our parents, and for others outside of our familial bonds. Our femininity was constructed, and we became. And where Ntsiki, quoted in the epigraph, is concerned, hers is a plan to become acceptable, take people's comfort into consideration, be a good Christian woman, and still enjoy a life and a personality outside of Christian boundaries.

This research project investigates the role of religion in legitimating social constructs and ideologies (Argyle 2000), specifically in the construction of femininity – while taking into account the means and strategies through which women in these religious settings negotiate, resist, or embody these constructs. Sermons from four Pentecostal Charismatic churches in Alexandra are analysed to find which aspects of womanhood are discussed by each of the pastors, and through post-sermon discussions I probe how women such as Ntsiki respond to the sermons and relate them to wider societal settings. Two of the churches, God's Love and Red Sea Ministries, are pastored by women – Pastor Fuzeka Nomfalweni (referred to as Pastor Fuzeka) and Pastor Xolile Shabangu (referred to as Pastor Xoli) respectively.[1] The other two churches are pastored by men with the assistance of their wives, who are also ordained as pastors. They are Upper Hall Ministries, led by Bishop Luvuyo Silawuli, and Living Waters, led by Pastor Petrus Nyathi. I write about these churches both in their individual capacities and as a group. A group in that the four churches, and their pastors, come together for ceremonies, what I call 'special services', on Holy dates such as the Easter weekend. Resources they share on these special days also include worship leaders – like Nkuli, pictured in figure 1.1, whose father is Bishop Silawuli – decorative items and musical instruments.

Pentecostal history: Identity re/formations

The Pentecostal group of churches is the fastest growing in the world and has a considerable following in Africa (Anderson 2013; Anderson & Otwang 1993; Isichei 2004). It is traced back in history to Azusa Street, Los Angeles, where William Seymour, the son of freed slaves, began a revival called the Apostolic Faith Mission in 1906. This group was racially integrated and had women in its leadership. It has been described as a movement that offered equality to the 'marginalised and dispossessed' (Anderson 2013: 43). The mission grew rapidly, spreading to 50 countries in 2 years. It was missionaries from Azusa Street who first introduced Pentecostalism into Africa when they preached and founded churches in Liberia and Angola. Many others were to follow, including the Apostolic Faith Mission (1913), Assemblies of God (1938) and Bethesda (1970), all founded in South Africa. The Zionist movement also contributes significantly to Pentecostal history in Southern Africa and is known for its resistance to white dominance and its efforts to indigenise Christianity (Anderson 2013; Isichei 2004).

New Pentecostals or Charismatics, which are the focus of my study, constitute independent branches of Pentecostalism. They are 'fast becoming a major expression of Christianity in Africa' (Anderson & Otwang 1993: 180) and attract a young, educated and urban generation. Charismatic Pentecostalism in South Africa saw its greatest rise with the country's transition to democracy. However, the big Charismatic churches were already beginning to engage with the politics of the late 1980s. Churches like Rhema, under Ray McCauley, were part of the 'Rustenburg Declaration' (1990) – admitting to a silent complicity with the atrocities of apartheid instead of being the Christian voice that spoke out against it (Anderson 2005, 2018). Another church, His People, expressed the desire for a non-racial church and country when it changed its logo to a photograph of a black hand and a white hand in a position of prayer, and incorporated symbolism into its church culture that reaffirmed Nelson Mandela's and Desmond Tutu's vision of a rainbow nation (Czeglédy 2008).

Religion, and Christianity more specifically, has been seen as a means through which political identities and new forms of nationalism are forged (Corten & Marshall-Fratani 2001; Miller & Yamamori 2007). But the new South Africa did not turn out to be all that was promised for all people, and Charismatic churches positioned themselves as a means to remedy the disillusionment or bitterness of different groups of South Africans. An indifference and resistance to the rapid changes the country was going through were accompanied by a leaning towards a blessing-theology on the part of many white Pentecostal Charismatic churches, whose members also continue to re-image themselves as travelling missionaries by planting churches in the countries to which they migrate (Anderson 2005). However, identity re/formations and a disillusionment with the country are not limited to white South Africans. In fact, the Charismatic movement throughout Africa is described by Chizobam Ruth Isichei as providing 'community confidence and hope in an age where independence has brought suffering and disappointment' (2004: 219). This provides us with a general view of the importance of Charismatic Christianity to its followers, but my interest is specifically in the women who attend these churches, which are largely populated by women.

Previous research on Africa and Latin America has attributed the attractiveness of Charismatic Pentecostalism for women to the modernising of the global south and to the 'coping mechanisms' it offers (James 2019; Martin 2003; McElhinny 2003). The Charismatic movement is seen by some scholars as a modernising instrument for women adapting to the 'fast and furious economic, social, and cultural changes imposed on them by forces not of their own making' (Martin 2003: 54). For other scholars, Charismatic Christianity is a haven for women as they grapple with what it means to be modern and learn middle-class behaviour (Frahm-Arp 2010; Sjørup 2002). Pentecostalism is described by John Burdick (1990) as a space for women to articulate their domestic concerns and by Elizabeth Brusco (1986, 2010) and David Stoll (1990) as a women's movement that aims to domesticate men. For Andrew Chesnut (1997), the Charismatic movement's focus on healing is what attracts women as the main caretakers of family and home. All of these reasons speak to women's relation to God, society and the self – and cannot be separated from their womanhood. As Annelin Eriksen suggests, Pentecostal space is made of 'gendered values'. Most of the literature I have just cited asks the questions: 'why are women so numerically dominant in these churches, and why do men still hold on to leadership positions' (Eriksen 2014: 1). Such a focus limits the question of gendered values, as it assumes rather than questions what it means to be a woman, occupy the spaces of femininity, and realise a gendered identity.

I step away from such assumptions in several ways. Firstly, I enter this research space as a subjective and embodied voice within the Charismatic Christian movement. Mine is a situated reading of the discourses that aim to fashion us as women coming into and also having grown up in the Charismatic practice. I also enter this space as an African feminist and womanist, interested in the complex, the nuanced and the historicised ways that intersect to create and influence gendered discourses. I use the plural 'discourses' because I argue that Charismatic Christianity is a contested space that does not neatly fit the binaries of a masculine versus feminine identity. Further, the multiple, sometimes paradoxical ways in which the women who have participated in this study interact with these discourses and create their own contradict the rigid assumptions of many Pentecostal scholars about feminine identities. This multiplicity should come as no surprise to anyone who has an interest in gender studies, and to any woman who has lived, breathed and become. Nonetheless, I state this position as an entry into my centring of Black women and their experiences within and outside their Charismatic churches. Finally, my embodiment of African Pentecostal beliefs and practices is not without questions and contentions – far from it. In a Black feminist politics of necessity, I critique the Charismatic churches I enter, mindful that 'it is how we choose to "be" within and amongst our differences that will make the ultimate difference between our ability to cut to heal versus cutting to bleed' (Dillard 2003: 231).

Black feminist theology

I begin my framing of Black women in affiliation to Black feminist theology as one expression of African feminism in relation to religion. This framework is important not only because of its focus on the context and experiences of women (Phiri 2004; Weems 1991) but also for its acknowledgement of many Black women's choices in aligning their spirithood to the Christian experience (Masenya 1994; Nadar 2009a).

Emerging in South Africa in 1982, Black feminist theology identifies Black women as the most oppressed and marginalised group in South Africa (Jordaan 1987; Landman 1995; Masenya 1995), thereby giving them 'a greater claim to God's compassion' (Jordaan 1987: 42). The movement comprises women within academia, various churches and South African Black society. It is a theology of liberation stemming from Black theology that centres Black women: it is based on 'both their intellectual capacity as well as their inner strength from their gut feelings' (Jordaan 1987: 45). Numerous academic articles and essays have been published in line with Black feminist theology using other names for this epistemology.

One example is the writings of Madipoane Masenya, who theorises and suggests a direction for feminist liberation hermeneutics. She argues for a feminist reading of the Bible as a remedy for its historical use as a tool to oppress women (Masenya 1995). More specifically, for Masenya, the Bible is to be read from the perspective of a Black woman's experience 'with a view to making her embrace the reality of God as liberator' (1994: 43). She maintains that Black women's experiences can challenge different forms of oppression based on race, gender, class and sexuality – unlike Black liberation movements, which challenge only racial discrimination, and dominant Western feminist theories, which focus only on gender discrimination (see also Crenshaw 1989; Gqola 2001, 2017b; Grant 2004; Phillips 2006). Following Alice Walker (1983) and Chikwenye Okonjo Ogunyemi (1985), Masenya thus moves from Black feminist theology to a womanist theology – which is termed, in keeping with the South African context, 'Bosadi' (Womanhood) theology. The Bosadi approach addresses the tension between the authority of the Bible and the authority of Black women (Masenya 1997b, 2005). In 'Biblical

Authority and the Authority of Women's Experience: Whither Way?' (1999), Masenya challenges established biblical scholarship to research Black women's everyday lived experiences and foreground the liberating elements of the Bible that can address these experiences. Sarojini Nadar (2005a, 2005b) and Rosinah Mmannana Gabaitse (2012, 2015) take up this challenge through a womanist hermeneutics that addresses the lived experiences of South African and Botswanan women. Their womanist framework incorporates a (re)reading of the spirit, which is a major expression and definition of the Pentecostal experience, as liberation and empowerment for women rather than holding them to gendered boundaries (see also Casselberry 2008; Pierce 2013).

I, in taking up the challenge posed by the Bosadi framework to centre religious Black women's experiences, do not do this as a theologian or a scholar of the Bible but rather as an interdisciplinary percipient of religious communities. Mine is not to engage in a systematic study of the divine, but to employ the invaluable womanist (re)interpretation/s of biblical texts and spirituality already outlined. I read in our shared epistemologies the important feature of 'narrative knowing' (see Nadar 2019) that recognises the importance of Black women's stories in research, teaching and learning. In this way, the narratives of the women to whom I speak and about whom I write evidence their experiences, their knowledge and *their own* interpretations of biblical discourse.

Womanism, Black feminism and African feminism

I do not wish to privilege the naming of my feminism with any label and find no obligation to do so. The stance I take is that of a Black woman, already intersectional and bringing to the fore the experiences of Black women from my community. As Pumla Dineo Gqola states:

> There are many feminist strands, which is to say different kinds of feminism, there are also many core principles. The commitment to actively oppose and end patriarchy is one. The recognition that

> patriarchy works like other systems of oppression,
> like racism and capitalism, to value some people
> and brutalise others is another area of agreement.
>
> (2017b: 56)

Hence my utilising of the terms womanism, Black feminism and African feminism. As a collective of theories brought to the flesh, I use the term Blackwomen to identify this rich scholarship (see Gqola 2017b). We all have in common the social justice for which we stand, our centring of the experience of Black women no matter what, and our bringing of our own experiences as evidence of the embodied truth that we bring to scholarship. How we name ourselves is important in as far as it allows us to take responsibility for the labels we choose, instead of accepting labels that have been given to us and forced on our kind for centuries (Gqola 2001). I borrow from all Black woman-centred feminisms the wealth of theory that brings forth my writing for those who, like myself, exist in social and spiritual spaces that give us some of the liberation we yearn for but are still in need of change. In doing so, I bring the flesh of Black Pentecostal women into the theory of Blackwomen scholarship, and I do not shy away from the centring of my own experiences as well, for

> Black women's scholarship has placed Black
> women and their experiences at the center of
> analysis just like traditional White men's scholarship
> has placed White men and their experiences at the
> center of analysis; the crucial difference is that
> Black women's scholarship has articulated and
> owned the centering, whereas traditional White
> men's scholarship has not.
>
> (Phillips & McCaskill 2006: 88)

So I forge a reading of the women with whom I congregate and whom I study as a means to tell our story with a responsibility to engagement and change, and to illuminate the meaning of everyday experiences as a legitimate source of knowledge (Dillard 2000).

Entry points

The chapter to follow provides a review of research on Pentecostal Charismatic churches in Africa. I name it 'Contested Pentecostalisms: A Review' to highlight the contestations that exist in Pentecostal practices and in the scholarly views of Pentecostals, too. The chapter is laid out according to the main themes and most prevalent research topics that comprise the scholarship on African Pentecostal churches. I also note how, even within these contestations, the current scholarship on born again Christians is a flattened view that presents Pentecostals only in the setting of the megachurch, and relies on an over-emphasis on the prosperity gospel. Scholarship on born again women also (rightfully) identifies the subjugation of the feminine but, in South Africa especially, does not apply a Black feminist framework that gives the voice back to the women under study.

Hence my employment and discussion – in Chapter 3, 'Between the Feminised Other and Black Women's Power' – of Blackwomen theory that historicises, contextualises and links discourses to practice. This chapter is a reading of the theory that I bring to the flesh of Black women in my study of the constructions of femininity in Pentecostal churches in Alexandra township. Not only does this chapter discuss the complexities of taking on gendered identities, it also insists on recognising and finding the voice of the Black woman in a way that does not other and objectify her. For it is another responsibility of Blackwomen scholarship to find a voice in women which was always within them (Collins 2000). Further, in line with the suggestion by Judith Casselberry and Elizabeth Pritchard, 'to study Pentecostals in general, and Black Pentecostal women in particular, requires... *sensitivity to the full range of power's frequencies*: persuasive and coercive, material and spiritual, subtle and palpable, hidden and ostentatious, injurious and expansive, exploitative and accountable (Casselberry & Pritchard 2019: 12, emphasis my own). I enter this space of research and report to counteract the discussion of femininity that lies solely along the lines of power, structure and agency. I suggest, instead, that the feminine be seen as a multiplicity of relations, performativity, will and 'flesh'.

It is on this basis that I write my entry into Chapter 4, 'This Field I Call Home'. My discussion of my 'native' and (auto) ethnographic standing within the community I study describes my ethical considerations, analysis and the building of relationships with my participants. I also explain why I utilise dialogue: not just in the sense of 'formalised' interviews, but as 'conversations'. Conversing is essential for challenging one's preconceptions, and also challenges the researcher to create new ways of 'being' a researcher (Dillard 2000). This choice of methodology not only justifies my researching a field of familiarity, but expresses my feminist commitment and responsibility to attending to the language, voice and experiences of women with whom I strongly identify.

In Chapter 5, 'Constructions of Femininity', I begin by placing the setting of the churches I study within the township of Alexandra: the different modes of transport I utilise, the people I come across, and Alexandra's various textures, colours and smells. Contextualising Alexandra, its culture and history, is important. Alexandra is the sole surviving 'freehold' Black township in South Africa, which means that even during apartheid Black and coloured people had land rights and were somewhat protected from the impeding Land Acts and pass laws of a violently racialised and unjust system (Bonner & Nieftagodien 2008; Mayekiso 1996).[2] However, the township's identity as a farming and entrepreneurial space later became complicated by slum dwellers who, fleeing the forced removals resulting from the implementation of the Land Acts, found solace and home in an urban area occupied by their own. Being a space that was unregulated and without close white supervision, Alexandra attracted even more people, including immigrants from the then Rhodesia and other Southern African countries. The township grew rapidly in the years from 1938 to 1944, but more importantly began to gain what Phillip Bonner and Noor Neiftagodien describe as 'multiple personalities' (2008). It was a combination of all these personalities, the complaints of drunkenness and wild parties by white neighbours in the surrounding suburbs, and a rising rate of crime that earned Alexandra its pseudonym, Gomora.[3]

Within Gomora there are many individuals who attend mainline and Pentecostal churches every Sunday.[4] In Chapter 5 I visit four Pentecostal Charismatic churches that are scattered around Alexandra. I then analyse the sermons that are delivered by their pastors, noting the views they provide of femininity to shape and challenge the spirituality of the women congregants and their relationship with God. More importantly, I provide a narrative analysis of the responses of the women who attend these churches. Their experiences uncover an interplay between submission and wilfulness that points to the need to further study the paradox of Pentecostal femininity. I argue that the constructions of femininity and gendered identity in these churches produce an unresolved tension between normative views of womanhood and challenges to them from a broadly modern feminist standpoint. What is most interesting about my findings is that this unresolved tension plays itself out in terms of different and conflicting understandings of spirituality and its feminine embodiments.

Lastly, in Chapter 6, I attend to the 'Question of Difference'. This concluding chapter is my love letter to African Pentecostal women and an ode to Audre Lorde. In it I probe the marking of difference through which Pentecostal women in Alexandra define their femininities. This may be a way to attend to the centre of Blackwomaness, I suggest, and finally root out the oppression that comes from outside but stubbornly resides within.

Figure 1.1. Nkuli Silawuli, worship leader.
Source: Exaltation Facebook page, https://web.facebook.com/ExaltationCrew/photos/pb.100063472213462.-2207520000./1110380969044716/?type=3, accessed 22 October 2022.

Chapter 2

Contested Pentecostalisms: A review

They once had this show about *amaPK* [Pastors' Kids]. That was such a bad representation of PKs because they only went for the ones who are loud and crazy and love to party: like the one girl who would spend *bo ma 5k on utshwala* [about R5 000 on alcohol]. I mean, there are many of us *angithi* [right], Tumi? Some of us are calm and we listen to our music at home. So many different personalities but they only showed South Africa the crazy PKs!

– Thando, 32-year-old electrical engineer, mother of one

Have you read the Comaroffs?

After presenting my research at a workshop in 2019, some of the senior academics were surprised at my not having cited the Comaroffs. And they took it that I did not mention these celebrated scholars because I had no knowledge of them. Referring to Madipoane Masenya to ground my theory in an understanding of Black feminist theology and displaying the alignment of my research questions with the theorising of African feminism was not quite to their academic taste – not without the Comaroffs.

I have read the Comaroffs, as I have read many other scholarly articles and books on the African Pentecostal movement, and this chapter stands as proof of my scholarly receipts. Jean and John Comaroff are not scholars of African Pentecostalism, but enter the academic conversations on Pentecostalism to further their theories of the 'occult economies' of contemporary capitalism (Comaroff & Comaroff 1999). So, having mentioned the Comaroffs, in the rest of this chapter I focus on the scholarly work on African Pentecostal Charismatic churches published over the past 20 or so years, in a broad overview of a very vast body of literature, which I have necessarily to summarise.

Looking at the literature based mainly on research conducted in Ghana, Nigeria, the Democratic Republic of the Congo, Botswana, Kenya, the Ivory Coast and South Africa, this review is organised to show the main trends in recent literature on African Pentecostalism and the key topics covered by it. I must note that most of the literature is biased towards a homogeneous identity of Pentecostalism as a picture of the megachurch and the many miracle-focused pastors that have dominated the media lately. My focus is on smaller churches, based in Alexandra township. I show throughout this book that these churches add layers to Pentecostal practice that are overlooked by scholarship on African Pentecostalism.

I begin with a discussion of the prosperity gospel and how it has been viewed by different scholars. Charismatic Christians have been associated with prosperity and the desire for it, and a review of different viewpoints gives us an idea of how Pentecostal Charismatic churches construct prosperity around an upwardly mobile congregation and their negotiation with past traditions and family. I then review the literature on the relationship between Charismatic churches and different media. The way in which media are appropriated by, and in turn appropriate, the culture of Charismatics gives insight into the Pentecostal agenda to change, shape and affect the world. Lastly, and closer to the focus of this book, I provide a review of Pentecostal gendered discourses. Here I discuss how scholarship has represented the gendered discourses of African Charismatics and how they affect the women and men who follow them.

The concluding remarks will focus on one scholar and her book as an example of how views of a movement can be distorted by one's positionality. I also note that some room is made for diversity and complexity in African Pentecostal literature. But this literature is still mostly directed at the megachurches, and exposes the shortcomings resulting from the positionality and limitations of researchers. Lastly, I show not only my contribution to this vast and growing literature, but also how my own positionality and knowledge of the language of my participants layers African Pentecostal scholarly accounts in a new way.

Upward mobility, breaking from the past and the prosperity gospel

In literature and in the media, Pentecostal Charismatic churches have often been referred to as prosperity churches – with assertions made of a direct link between their theology and practices and the prosperity gospel, which claims material, this-worldly success as a sign of divine grace (Heuser 2016; Quayesi-Amakye 2011). This is associated with claims that hope and blessings are received by those who give generous offerings and tithe loyally to the church (Coleman 2000; Gifford 2007). Tracing the origins of this message to North American Christianity (Gifford 1990; Hunt 2000; Mbewe 2011), many agree that the narrative of 'health and wealth' has found a home in Africa and other parts of the global south (Anderson 2002; Chesnut 2012; Coleman 2011; Gbote & Kgatla 2014; Hasu 2006; Hendricks 2019; Hunt 1995; Kroesbergen 2014).[5]

So ensues the debate on what Pentecostalism embodies within the rhetoric and practice of so-called 'health and wealth ministries' (Bishau 2013). On the one hand, the Pentecostal movement is bemoaned for taking advantage of the poor with the promise of immediate and magical enrichment (Asamoah-Gyadu 2015; Dube 2019) and for further entrenching the structural violences of inequality (Deacon & Lynch 2013). On the other hand, Pentecostalism is aligned with Max Weber's Protestant ethic. This interpretation argues for Pentecostalism's promotion of individual success and socioeconomic development (Berger 2008; CDE South Africa 2008; Freeman 2012; Togarasei 2011), especially by responding to commercial, skills-related urban needs (Haynes 2012; Togarasei 2005). Not all accounts of this version of Pentecostalism paint it in a negative light. For instance, John F. McCauley (2012) suggests that a patronage system is formed through Pentecostalism, which closes the economic and social network gaps left by governments. Ann Bernstein and Stephen Rule (2010) note that Charismatic Christians in South

Africa report having gained confidence and agency through their conversion, by learning the importance of entrepreneurship and gaining administrative skills from volunteering at their churches. Maria Frahm-Arp adds that His People Christian Church (a megachurch in Johannesburg) has business-focused networks that not only build a supportive community for young aspirant entrepreneurs, but also encourage entering the business world as a means of changing South Africa for the better (Frahm-Arp 2010). As both Allan Anderson and Frahm-Arp underscore, the same entrepreneural culture driven by an encouragement of hard work is promoted by the Grace Bible Church (a Soweto-based megachurch), which caters for a new Black middle class, publicly distances itself from the prosperity gospel, and merges African values with Western traditions (Anderson 2018; Frahm-Arp 2010).

Comparing Charismatic churches in Kenya and South Africa, Deborah James (2019) sees a discourse that divorces the finances of 'the world' from those 'of God', encourages saving and tithing as opposed to a life of conspicuous consumption, and challenges the growing inequalities of the world while encouraging church members to be self-reflective in their newly acquired societal status. James (2019) and Birgit Meyer (2007) draw on epistomologies of Charismatics in Africa and find a general leaning towards the promotion of capitalism and forging middle classness. It is this drive towards a 'modern' way of life that constitutes a breaking from the past – often meaning a 'concomitant rejection of African culture' (Engelke 2010: 191). Problematising kinship and local ties is also seen as a born again experience that promises a triumph over the believers' ailments and poverty (Engelke 2004; Laurent 2001; Marshall-Fratani 1998; Meyer 1998, 1999, 2004; Van Dijk 1992, 1998).

However, according to Sasha Newell (2007), the link between African traditions, the Pentecostal movement and modernity is more complex than a born again breaking from the past. Newell argues that the Pentecostal movement in Africa speaks to the needs and beliefs of its members through a witchcraft discourse that 'at once fits pre-existing religious beliefs about efficacy against witchcraft and access to material prosperity...while at the same time correspond[ing] to an...interest in modernity' (2007:

472). Newell therefore identifies similarities between Pentecostal and traditional African discourses, arguing that both are directed towards a moral capitalism. In a related argument, he writes that Ivory Coast communities are as suspicious and in awe of the successes of Pentecostal churches as they are of the success of the secular government officials and businessmen (Newell 2007).

In her book *Professional Women in South African Pentecostal Charismatic Churches* (2010), Maria Frahm-Arp gives an account of megachurches in Johannesburg, which, she contends, have in common a growing middle class of professionals but differ in their stances on capitalism and prosperity, and also in their versions of upward mobility and 'breaking from the past'. So, while Grace Bible Church and His People are in agreement on the nuclear family as a good model of the modern Christian home, the Soweto-based Grace Bible Church still upholds African values, such as the importance of lobola and taking care of the extended family, whereas His People encourages a complete 'Western-like' break away from all traditional African practices.

Pentecostals in Africa are often seen to be politically involved and motivated, as upward mobility is also associated with a strong sense of citizenship, including in the form of active political participation (Haynes 2018; Patterson & Kuperus 2016; Sperber & Hern 2018). But Pentecostal Charismatic churches' practices and attitudes towards upward mobility, including engagement with party politics, differ vastly. Frahm-Arp (2015b) shows that Pentecostal churches took on different forms of political involvement during South Africa's 2014 elections, depending on their communities and on what it was felt would benefit them. Frahm-Arp's analysis of the sermons and social media pages of three churches reveals similarities in that congregants were encouraged to be responsible, politically involved members of society by voting and praying for the leaders of the country. However, the churches took on different intensities of involvement regarding which party to support. One of the churches stated that people should make a 'Godly' choice when selecting a leader, and held an open debate on Facebook about which political party was best and why. Another church invited leaders of different political parties to address church members as a means to have an influence over the country's governance. And the third church had a direct involvement with the ruling party so that members could gain access to municipal grants and break the chains of unemployment and hopelessness.

Lovemore Togarasei (2015) sees the involvement of Charismatic churches in all aspects of this-worldliness as a move towards the secularisation of religion. Secularisation is evident in how Pentecostal churches have 'undermined traditional values in favour of modern, secular values' (2015: 60). He mentions His People church as an example of how local pop culture (*kwaito* sounds specifically) and other secular forms are integrated into the practices of the church, and help to appeal to the values of the elite and those who aspire to be part of it. Togarasei further discusses how the practices and discourses of Pentecostals secularise Christianity. Pentecostals lean to the secular in their focus on the rewards of this world rather than on those of the life to come, including in their use of gospel music, which Togarasei contends only differs from pop culture in its lyrics, and also in their media usage as a means to build the image of Pentecostalism as a 'travelling religion'.

Even though there are obvious complexities in scholars' accounts of African Pentecostalism, there is a tendency to view the Charismatic movement in binary terms. Discussions of the prosperity gospel are either in favour of or against this hermeneutic. Upward mobility is shown as a desire of all Pentecosal congregants, and one that is closely tied to a modern identity that includes breaking ties with African traditions and problematising familial relations. All of these views are also based on a focus on megachurches in Africa, shutting out the voices and identities of churches and congregants that may not share these views. All the scholars I have reviewed agree that Pentecostalism is growing rapidly and may be representing the main trajectory of Christianity in Africa, but to produce an accurate and inclusive account of how this representation is taking form requires that the views and identities of rural, township (and Grace Bible Church is not the only township Charismatic church) and all other spatial locations be included in theorising. With more layered research, we may come to uncover more possibilities for making sense of the growing influence of the Charismatic movement in South Africa and the rest of the continent, and the intricate ways in which the congregants engage with its practices.

Mediated Pentecostalism and shaping 'the world'

Several studies have shown that Pentecostals in many parts of the African continent appropriate the media to reach and appeal to people and change how people are receiving and perceiving religion, and how they connect to it (Hackett 1998; Khanyile 2016; Parsitau & Mwaura 2010). Imagining the media as the modern form of letters that the Apostles in Early Christian times sent out even from the confines of prison cells, Pentecostal Charismatic churches justify their use of television, print media, radio, emails, bumper stickers and the internet as a necessary course of action to reach out to the world (Adogame 2008; Togarasei 2012).

Marlene de Witte (2003) illustrates how Charismatic churches dominate the Ghanaian airwaves, as they are well placed to purchase airtime from television and radio broadcasters. The pastors not only host their own shows, affiliated to their churches, but some of them have achieved celebrity status as they are interviewed for entertainment, hired to present radio and television gospel shows, and paid to speak on special occasions.

Francis Benya (2018) and Ogbu Kalu (2010) see the Charismatic churches in Ghana as a 'marketplace' that utilises the media to commercialise religion. Messages are packaged as religious products, and marketing strategies are also used to sell goods such as books, videos and more. Through billboards, television and radio advertisements, Ghanaian churches show off their product value and beckon to their communities to join them in prayer meetings, concerts and special services. Olive oil producers have also taken to Pentecostalism, using famous pastors to market their brands as the much demanded 'anointing oil' (Asamoah-Gyadu 2005).

The churches in Alexandra township that I discuss in this book have no direct 'reach' to the world through mediated engagements, but rather encourage their members to attract others to the life of Christianity by setting themselves apart. Their pastors are more concerned with the individual conduct of their members, and their sermons are mostly directed at that.

These pastors also strongly condemn the purchase of oils or any other product promising to increase blessing. The practices they encourage are geared towards spiritual challenges that they wish their congregants to undertake.

Even in scholarship, the relationship between the media and Pentecostalism is not reported as one-sided. According to Birgit Meyer (2006: 300), the entertainment domain is not only adopted by Pentecostalism but 'parasitically thrives on' it, too. She argues that popular Ghanaian video films appropriate the Pentecostal concepts of vision in their narratives as 'revelations', and in their positioning of the viewer as the bearer of a priviledged knowledge that is yet to be revealed to the protagonist. While it may seem boring to some, this style of film has been found to be popular amongst Ghanaian Pentecostal women, who see the films as a visual support to the Sunday sermons (Verrips 2002). It has also been noted that audiences for Nigerian and Ghanaian video films appreciate the Christian moral code in these movies as an affirmation of their devotional views. In 'Business of the Spirit: Ghanaian Broadcast Media and the Commercial Exploitation of Pentecostalism', De Witte (2011) ascribes the Pentecostal character of the media to the born again identity of the owners and managers of different media houses in Ghana. So, even though Ghanaian legislation does not permit the existence of religious stations, the convictions of management are still communicated through their broadcasts (2011: 196–197). This places the media regulators in the difficult situation of balancing freedom of expression against respect for all religions and beliefs, which is made especially difficult by dominant Charismatics openly criticising other religions, and African religiosity especially.

In Kinshasa, celebrities depict themselves as 'Christian artists'. Katrien Pype (2009) describes how the definition of what makes a celebrity is influenced by Charismatic moral codes, which place the audience in the position of creating the reputation of performers from a Christian point of view. Christian artists are considered more moral, less susceptible to demonic possesion, and in possession of a Charismatic power that gives them access to secret knowledge. In Uganda, print, radio and television producers have reported that an inclusion of religious discourse and religious leaders increases their credibility and trust, because pastors are seen as opinion leaders (Bompani & Brown 2015). Consequently, editorial strategies in Uganda are in line with values connected with Pentecostal Charismatic churches. Pype underscores that journalists feel compelled to frame their writing in a 'moralistic discourse that seeks to encourage "good" individual and societal behavior that ties in with traditional and religious principles' (2012: 120).

Selome Igbekele Kuponu (2015) and Rosalind Hackett (2009) describe Pentecostal churches' websites as an extension of the megachurch buildings, and as enhancing the charisma of the leading pastors, too. The sites provide a space for visitors (Christian or otherwise) to interact with the message of the church without having to enter the building. They also provide access to interactive web pages where visitors can submit prayer requests, join the membership of the church and find a branch (Asamoah-Gyadu 2007b). Yet, though other mediated forms of Pentecostalism allow for control of the churches' identities and chosen direction, entry into social media complicates this for them. Femi J. Kolapo (2019) looks at the social media pages and handles of some prominent churches in Nigeria and finds that their following is not just made up of members or admirers of the churches. Social media is used to question the ethics of Pentecostal Charismatic churches, especially in the context of the prosperity gospel, with concerns raised about Charismatic pastors' lack of transparency. Kolapo (2019) emphasises, however, that push-back from those who support the pastors under scrutiny is just as strong as the criticism.

Sphesihle Khanyile describes the use of social media by miracle-focused Pentecostal churches as an 'appropriation for the focal projects of evangelization and visibility' (2017: 49). Khanyile delves into the use of social media to advance the discourse of these churches, drawing on the Facebook page of Prophet Penuel Mnguni's End Times Disciple Ministries as a case study. What interests me are Khanyile's findings regarding the representation of women by the church. Images of women eating snakes, stripping to show that the temperature of the room has miraculously increased, stood upon by the prophet, and eating their weaves are proudly posted on the page to show off the miraculous powers held by Prophet Mguni. Khanyile interprets this as a humiliating display of hegemonic power over the helpless, disposable and despised body of the Black woman. The churches I have visited, in contrast, do not have a large social or public media presence. God's Love, Alexandra, does however make use of some of Apostle Popela's God's Love Family Church's social media presence. Apostle Popela ordained Pastor Fuzeka and Pastor Patrick, and still plays an important role as their spiritual mentor. Nor are they focused on miracle healing. They are small community churches based in Alexandra township. I have also never seen any such morbid displays of power by any of the pastors, men or women. Nevertheless, the question of how sexuality, gender identity and femininities are constructed is still an important one for these churches.

Gendered ideologies and identities

Several studies have argued that Pentecostal women experience violence at the hands of men, and do not find the necessary support from the church to free themselves of it (Maluleke & Nadar 2002; Nadar 2005a, 2005b; Sande 2019). Frahm-Arp (2015a) attributes women's acceptance of domestic violence to systems of power within Pentecostalism that create an ideology of denial, normalising and self-blame. These are: surveillance – practised by women's groups within the churches; the pastorate – which through the insistence on submission and prayer makes the women believe that their experiences are their own fault; silencing – through shame and the perception of failing at being good Christian women; and a rigid, enforced (including by women leaders) view of patriarchy. These systems run through Grace Bible Church and the Zion Christian Church in such a consistent and dense manner that women who decide to end abusive relationships end up disassociating themselves from the church, too. Caroline Tuckey and Louise Kretzschmar (2002), who have conducted empirical research on the Church of the Province of Southern Africa in Johannesburg, argue that Pentecostalism 'preps' women and men for patriarchal structures that could lead to violence and oppression of women from a young age by socialising girls and boys for a Christian life of servitude and inferiority or dominance and macho leadership.

Patriarchal ideology is further entrenched throughout different stages of women's lives. Groups based on biblical descriptions of good women are formed to teach Pentecostal women to 'know their place' in society (Mate 2002: 5). This place is taken up in feminine roles that are set by the church. One of these roles is that of motherhood. Frahm-Arp (2016) draws a comparison between the idealised images of Christian motherhood and those of motherhood according to popular culture found in magazines and television commercials. She finds that the churches construct their ideals of motherhood based on pop culture discourse, and then legitimise this through an 'authoritative' reference to the Bible. The churches 'embrace these discourses of the nursing mother, the grooming mother, and the attentive mother' found in popular discourse and 're-code [them] as something deeply spiritual' (2016: 177). The female members internalise these roles and try to apply them to their lives. Careers for women are seen only as a temporary means of financial survival until such a time as God blesses the family by giving the husband an income that will allow him to take his rightful place as head and provider – and the wife hers as primary, stay-at-home family caregiver. The role of wife is linked closely to that of mother in that it is constructed as a service to the family, but introduces a relation of submission to a husband (Ellece 2011; KaNdlondlo 2011; Parsitau & Mwaura 2010).

Sarojini Nadar and Cheryl Potgieter term this ideology 'formenism' (Nadar & Potgieter 2010) and 'masculinism' (Nadar 2009b):

> Formenism, like masculinism, subscribes to a belief in the inherent superiority of men over women, but unlike masculinism it is not an ideology developed and sustained by men, but an ideology designed, constructed, and sustained by women. Like its phonetics suggests, this is a concept for men – that is to say, men are the chief beneficiaries of the hierarchical social positioning that it advocates.
>
> (Nadar & Potgieter 2010: 141)

In their analysis of Gretha Wiid's Worthy Women's Movement, Nadar and Potgieter (2010) find the use of psychologisation, pastoralisation and prophetisation as discourses employed to construct gender roles and encourage women towards a paradigm of for*men*ism. Wiid 'describes herself as a "finessekenner", or finesse expert…[she holds] conferences and especially school talks and camps on sex' (Nortjé-Meyer 2011: 2). One of the most popular conferences hosted by Wiid is the Worthy Women's Conference, where she gives South African women (especially in the Afrikaner community) advice on marriage.

By employing psychologisation, Wiid positions herself as an expert in psychology, well able to offer women advice and coping strategies; her use of pastoralisation places her in a unique position of God-given authority – even giving examples of her own submission to her husband. Nadar and Potgieter further illustrate how the position encouraged by Wiid appropriates John Stuart Mill's description of the 'willing slave', where subordination is a choice made by women fitting with institutional (religious in this case) requirements (Nadar and Potgieter 2010: 146). Women also accept for*men*ism because it offers the solution of 'patriarchal bargaining', where men are given leadership in exchange for being responsible for their wives and children (2010: 147). It is also worth noting that women receive no reward for their role in taking care of the family. Like Rosinah Mmannana Gabaitse (2012, 2015), whose research is based on Pentecostalism in Botswana, Nadar and Potgieter link the discourse of submission in South Africa to the abuse experienced by women in their relationships with men.

In defining masculinism, Nadar (2009b) refers to the Mighty Men's Conference (MMC), founded and led in South Africa by Angus Buchan. The movement claims to help men 'regain' their masculinity. Niel Vels (2013) reasons that the MMC appeals to the loss of identity experienced by Buchan's farming Afrikaner congregants. He likens it to a gang that offers the displaced a solution and an opportunity 'to help them make sense of life and their identity, particularly the sense of loss (and possible loss of identity) in tough economic and social circumstances' (2013: 124). These circumstances are the changes brought about by the transition from apartheid to democracy in South Africa. Democracy in Africa has also meant the empowerment of women, which has resulted in a relative transformation in gender relations. Ezra Chitando and Kudzai Biri (2013) see Pentecostal masculinity discourses as a response to these changes. They deliberate over the discourse of the Zimbabwe Assemblies of God Africa (ZAOGA) and how it teaches and encourages men to take up indigenous masculine roles as heads of their homes or risk having their wives take the reins. Loving and providing for their wives and children, as well as fixing broken appliances around the house, are part of this role, and help men to maintain their God-given positions in their families. Men at ZAOGA also keep their masculine identities by seeking out extramarital sexual partners when their wives fail to fulfil their feminine roles of satisfying them sexually, to ensure that they are not too 'stiff' to pray. Wives are also expected to pray for their husbands so that satanic women do not seduce them.

Other authors give a sense of male responsibilisation in the construction of masculinities by Pentecostalism. The born again experience requires men to leave behind the recklessness of substance abuse, promiscuity and violence in favour of a Christian life that takes male leadership and agency as caring, considerate and loving within the home (Pype 2012; Soothill 2007; Van Klinken 2011, 2012), as well as taking on roles in sociopolitical spheres (Van Klinken 2016). Martin Lindhardt (2015) notes that in Tanzanian Pentecostalism a negotiated masculinity allows for a reformed, harmonious private life balanced with power and respectability in public. Marian Burchardt (2018) also acknowledges the responsibility element in the construction of Pentecostal masculinity, but in addition highlights an element of traditional masculinity. These 'fundamentally contradictory' constructs lead to the assumption that 'Pentecostal masculinity may rise to become a new hegemony rather than offering ways to escape, or reproducing hegemonic masculinity', especially since 'Pentecostalism is increasingly seen as the religion of "success"' (Burchardt 2018: 123).

Control of sexual desire is another agenda of some Charismatic churches in Africa. Being born again means successfully abstaining from sex until after one is married or risking being barred from the church (Parsitau 2009). Couples are also to remain loyal to each other, and polygamy is not tolerated, so men are taught self-control and women seduction to keep their husbands interested in them (Pearce 2012; Quiroz 2016). In Botswana, counselling is considered an important practice amongst the upwardly mobile members as a means to receive sexual education, be prepared for marriage and learn about HIV and AIDS (Van Dijk 2013). Pentecostal Charismatic churches in sub-Saharan Africa only recognise heterosexual relations, and see any form of plurality as a sin and a betrayal of African identity (Van Klinken & Obadare 2018), but LGBTQI+ movements are challenging this stance by claiming recognition and are also becoming more visible in communities.[6] Still, in her study of a Pentecostal group in Cape Town, Melissa Hackman (2018) discovers that control of the body is taught to 'ex-gay men' through 'desire work', as a means of moving them away from their feminised same-sex desire to a respectable masculinity that promises God-given power and leadership.

Women's bodies are controlled within church structures through dress, submission to men and authorities, and a restraint they must practise even within the Pentecostal space, where the spirit may lead congregants to exuberant dancing and singing. This is the case in some of the churches I have visited in Alexandra township, and is especially the case for single women in Nairobi who, according to Damaris Parsitau (2020), submit to protect themselves from violence and criticism. Gregory Deacon and Gabrielle Lynch (2013) and Parsitau (2009, 2020) discuss whether Pentecostalism is empowering or subordinating for women in Kenya, and come to the conclusion that it does both. Similar complexities are highlighted by Johnson Kwabena Asamoah-Gyadu (2007a), who analyses the combative prayers against barrenness in a Ghanaian church. The women and men who attend these services are broken and shamed by a tradition that does not accept childlessness in marriage, and look to the church for assurance and healing from shame. Patrick Claffey (2007), similarly, sees some of the processes followed during these prayer sessions as humiliating to the couples who subject themselves to them. Asamoah-Gyadu adds that the prayer camps, even though they offer solutions to African traditional problems, do not have empathy towards the childless and only serve to increase their pain, especially since they denounce adoption.

Referring to them as the 'fantastic fetus', Nathanael Homewood (2018) sees the miracle babies conceived after such prayer camps as 'super citizens' of Ghanaian Pentecostalism. On the one hand, the divine citizenship of the fetus challenges the autonomy, agency and citizenship of the mother by defining her identity as a mere 'fetal incubator' (2018: 628). On the other hand, however, the identity of the fetal carrier can be seen as elevated to that of divine carrier, and working directly with God in the miraculous act of creation.

Pentecostal discourse has also been found to construct female identity as spiritually gifted and religiously sensitive (Cazarin & Griera 2018; Martin 2003; Sackey 2006), qualities that justify positions of leadership, pastoral included, for women. But a strong distinction is still made between what liberties and authority women may enjoy in church and their expected submission at home and in other societal settings (Cazarin & Griera 2018). Scholars lament the lesser numbers of ordained female leaders in Pentecostal spaces in spite of the fact that the beliefs of Pentecostalism are based on a democratic practice of spirituality and respect for spiritual gifts, regardless of class, gender or race (see Crawley 2008; Dube 2007; Nadar 2005b). Musa Dube (2014) agrees with Charles Barfoot and Gerald Sheppard (1980), connecting the failure to have more women ordained in Pentecostal circles with the 'Weberian theory which holds that new religions of the oppressed are characterised by gender equality in their beginnings, but the equality hardly lasts beyond the first stages of the formation of such communities' (Dube 2014: 3).

Where there are women leaders ordained as pastors, most are married to founders of Charismatic churches (Mapuranga 2013). Most also follow the discourse of formenism (Mapuranga 2018; Mate 2002; Schenectady & Parsitau 2017). But others, like Elizabeth Wahome, founder of the Single Ladies Interdenominational Ministry (SLIM), address the stigmatisation of single women and give them a haven where they are recognised as community heroes (Schenectady & Parsitau 2017: 6–9). In Alexandra, the number of women who have their own churches is dwindling. Instead, there is an increase in the number of ordainments of women married to men pastors. But this is not a problem unseen by church leaders. My findings will show that pastors are addressing the issue of ordainment and encouraging more women to take up leadership roles.

Some African male pastors have also shown support for the different struggles faced by Black women in their congregations. They provide spaces for coping mechanisms and new subjectivities that change how the women view themselves in the church and society. The women in such churches are found to have a high self-worth (regardless of marital status). They are also equipped with the masculine skills of management in corporate spaces (Frahm-Arp 2010, 2012; Gilbert 2015).

As I have said, much African Pentecostal scholarship is narrowly based on the megachurch and does not sufficiently bring the voices of the congregants of Pentecostal churches into view. We also need to bring into our academic research a closer scrutiny of the positionalities that inform anthropological reports of Pentecostal churches and Pentecostal women, or risk making assumptions that have not been tested with the rigour and ethics that all the people and subjects we study deserve.

A problematic view

Ilana van Wyk's *The Universal Church of the Kingdom of God in South Africa: A Church of Strangers* (2014) is one example of such unethical scholarship. In her book, Van Wyk describes the Universal Church of the Kingdom of God in sensationalist detail. According to the Introduction, Van Wyk had heard about this church and some of its members during her time in South Africa as a master's student, and again in England as a PhD candidate. I wonder how the story of the church would have taken shape had she conducted her research in England, instead of studying the Durban community that she decribes as impoverished and riddled with superstitions and a preoccupation with 'dark forces'. Phukile, a member of the church and community, becomes Van Wyk's informant and the embodied performance of the scholar's image of the Universal Church of the Kingdom of God. Reading Van Wyk's descriptions and recollections of their conversations, Phukile comes across as incoherent at best and deranged at worst. Like the other members of the Universal Church of the

Kingdom of God, she fosters deep levels of distrust – these members believe that evil forces are always upgrading their technologies to increase the chances of the devil influencing their families, friends and even fellow members of the church, and to block their blessings through witchcraft. Van Wyk sees this as the reason the Universal Church of the Kingdom of God does not build communities and foster friendships between its members. To Van Wyk, the congregants of the church are more 'clients' than they are a community. They attend church services to purchase oils, water and other goods for blessings, give or pledge tithes and large amounts of money in different campaigns, exorcise demons that stand in the way of their financial, health and family blessings, and pray combatively to receive all that God has in store for them.

Reading this book and its reviews had me in a conflicted place between my personal misgivings about the Universal Church, the positive reviews of Van Wyk's anthropological work (see, for example, Kirsch 2015, Premawardhana 2015 and Van de Kamp 2016), the church leaders' scathing reactions to what they saw as her sloppy and generalised statements, and my unease at the sensationalist, reductive ways in which Van Wyk writes about her research participants.[7] It was listening to Van Wyk's keynote address at the 2020 GloPent Conference in Basel, Switzerland, that settled my conflict: I was right to feel uneasy, as she presented a view of Pentecostalism, South Africa's Black people and Black politicians that resembled the way she writes about Phukile. The keynote address was loaded with sensationalism, filled with sweeping statements and generalisations. She established a direct correlation between Black politicians, Black congregants and Black pastors' penchant for riches, witchcraft discourses and delirious actions that suggests that 'post-apartheid' South Africa is in a state of what she called 'spiritual schizophrenia'. When I asked her what evidence she could present to support her claims, Van Wyk quickly relented, claiming to have given her address based solely on accounts of 'commentators'. But she was unable to tell us about her own academic views. This does not surprise me, because serious academic research requires one to at the very least Google search a figure such as Andile Mngxitama and his political stance before concluding, as Van Wyk did, that his obviously Black name and face place him in a relationship with the controversial Prophet Bhushiri, in which the corrupt Black bandits band together in delirium and greed.

Conclusion

African Pentecostalism is a contested terrain that accommodates a multiplicity of practices and beliefs, as well as different and contrasting views of discourses of prosperity, gender, healing and the mediatisation of religion in Africa. The scholarship on Pentecostalism, however, is one-sided in terms of its focus on certain versions of Pentecostal beliefs and practices, with a strong bias towards megachurches. Many of the studies flatten complexity and reduce Pentecostalism and its numerous manifestations to a limited set of beliefs and practices. Others, like that of Van Wyk (2014), take this into the more dangerous territory of unethical, insensitive and factually dubious generalisations.

My work draws on sermons, practices and experiences from township Pentecostalism that do not necessarily represent the success and prosperity discourses so easily associated with Charismatic churches. Through this shift of focus, my research challenges many of the findings and assumptions of previous scholars who have focused on the mainstream(ed) African Pentecostalism of megachurches. In fact, my own positionality as a member of a Pentecostal church, and as a feminist scholar who is critical of many of the assumptions and hegemonic doctrines of mainstream African Pentecostalism, shows that existing literature has erased some of the complexities that define the experience of Pentecostalism for at least some of its followers. I foreground the experiences of Black women within a small group of churches in Alexandra township to close this gap.

Chapter 3

Between the feminised other and Black women's power

I fit in everywhere. I have all types of friends. Some of them drink and party and they know I don't but we can have a good time together. All of my friends, from slay queens to boMshoza, will come to my home and tell me about their lives. And I love them. They know I love them all.[8]

— Gloria, 40-year-old nursing assistant, mother of two

Ladies can be judgemental with each other, especially at church. But you can find a friend that makes you feel okay with yourself and with your mistakes. I have those types of friends here: who are like 'asikhulume, asiphileni' [let's talk, let's live]. [Tinyiko] is one of them, she reminds me that life isn't all about the law, and it goes beyond church – she reminds me to live. To have a woman in church who will lift you in prayer and also lift you in other aspects of your life is very important!

— Maria, 33-year-old cleaner, mother of three

Beyond the feminised other

If the literature on Pentecostal Charismatic churches in Africa that I reviewed in the previous chapter is anything to go by, then there is a pattern of gendered religious discourse that feminises the subjugated other. Even theologians call into question the role of Christianity in constructing an inferior identity for African women. Elijah M. Baloyi (2008a, 2008b, 2010) writes extensively about the hindrances that biblical interpretations pose to African women's rights by giving men undue control over their bodies. The same concerns regarding the subordination of African women are voiced by Renier Koegelenberg (2012), who studies masculinities as a means to curb the unequal power relations that cause women to be more vulnerable to HIV and AIDS infection, as they are unable to negotiate safe sex. Women, and Black women in particular, are amongst the poorest of the world's population and the most subjected to violence, even from their childhood. Ikenga Oraegbunam (2006) links the attitudes and beliefs that lead to the unfair biases against women to all of the major religions and cultural practices around the world, including Christianity. Women's identification with an inferior 'other' has also been attributed to the patriarchal imagery of God as subjugating male ruler, justifying men's 'natural' domination over women. Both men and women view and make sense of structures of society through this understanding (Daly 1985; Johnson 1984; Shooter 2014).

But these and other studies that highlight women's, and especially Black women's, subjugation present just one view of femininity. The feminine embodiment of culture, power relations and ideology can go beyond binary arguments for victim or victrix. When we investigate power networks and women's resistance to them, we must realise that 'this relationship is far more complex than a simple model of permanent oppressors and perpetual victims' (Collins 2000: 274). Having said this, I do not propose to completely abandon the issues of pain and internalised inferiority that have become so much part of Black women's constructed identity and of conversations about it, but I still want to nuance the Black female experience and her embodiment of the religious community in which she chooses to congregate.

That there can be an alternative to the Black African feminine identity of inferiority and subjugated other brings us to the discussion in this chapter of what gender identities are. This I undertake firstly by investigating the relations between religion, discourse, power and the law in order to historicise and map the creation of Black African women's gendered identities and how they are justified. These links also bring us to an understanding of how Black African women may have a hand in the embrace of oppressive power systems as they try to gain status and recognition. Embodiments bring us to an understanding of performativity as creating, sustaining, but also revealing the very fragility of respectable gender.

It is in this discussion of the strategic performances of gender that I bring in Judith Butler, as the only theorist cited in this chapter who is not a Blackwoman. I am aware that the oft-cited *Gender Trouble* (1990) by Butler was criticised by Paula M.L. Moya (1997) as having appropriated Cherrie Moraga (see Moraga & Anzaldua 1983) with the sole purpose of pushing a postmodernist agenda. Moya sees Butler's reading of Moraga as dismissive of 'the necessity of theorizing the connections between (and not simply ranking) the different kinds of oppression that people suffer' (Moya 1997: 134). Moya critiques postmodernity and Butler on the grounds that coming to a conclusion that the identity of the feminist 'subject' is 'unstable, shifting and contradictory' makes it difficult to account for experience and 'make[s] it difficult to figure out who is...the "oppressed" and who is the "oppressor"' (1997: 134).

I still choose to engage with Butler's theorising of gender as contradictory, unstable and shifting, in conversation with Danai Mupotsa's reading of the re/production of Black African women's gender in 'white weddings', as a necessary way of seeing and understanding Black African femininity in its incompleteness (Mupotsa 2014, 2015a, 2015b). Where this may seem paradoxical, there comes our responsibility as Blackwomen researchers to read the personal as political within the whispers of the subaltern. This close reading of paradoxes is one I deem vital to my attending to the fullness of Black African women's experiences.

African gender discourses: Religion, culture and the law

Sylvia Tamale (2014) relates Christian, Judaic and Islamic (which she groups as 'Messianic religious') texts to the current laws and policies in several African countries. Since in Africa there is a 'tendency...to adopt an institutionalised and organic union between religion and the state' (2014: 157), Tamale asserts a link between the three realms of the law, religion and culture, which she sees as working together to control African bodies. The control of bodies tends to weigh more heavily on women, as they are a means to the growth and sustenance of patriarchal capitalism. Men, who are often the heads of households, have economic power and control over women and children; and women free men to be active in industry and politics through the unpaid domestic labour of taking care of home and children. Keeping the domestic and public power bases this way means keeping women's sexuality under surveillance and creating laws with double standards for women and men. The laws on adultery are one such way of controlling African women and their bodies – ensuring the monogamy of women means that the paternity and legitimacy of children who are to inherit the wealth of a successful patriarch are not in question. And, of course, ensuring that it is male children who stand to inherit wealth also keeps this cycle going.

Tamale uses the term 'sexuality' to speak about

> a wide array of complex elements, including sexual knowledge, beliefs, values, attitudes and behaviours, as well as procreation, sexual orientation, and personal/interpersonal sexual relations. It touches a wide range of other issues, including pleasure, the human body, dress, self-esteem, gender identity, power and violence. It is an all-encompassing phenomenon that involves the human psyche, emotions, physical sensations, communication, creativity and ethics.
>
> (2014: 151)

And so, Tamale maintains that how and with whom we 'do' sexuality as Africans is largely influenced by religion, culture and the law. She also argues that the workings of these domains to uphold the political and economic status quo make their linkage a political one. Hence, she names the two largest religions in Africa – Islam and Christianity – 'political religions' and notes that they often set aside their differences in doctrine to come together in defence of conservative 'truths' on respectable sexuality.

Evangelical movements have a great influence on this perspective on sexuality, together with other Christian and Islamic movements and traditions. Marrying this conservative religious discourse to African culture and the law is how many Africans embody hegemonic discourses on sexual behaviour. It is also how Black African women (and men) who have 'failed' to uphold this set of moralistic discourses on sexuality are pushed to the periphery of society. Tamale uses former South African President Jacob Zuma's rape case as one example of how the embodiment of the Messianic 'punishment for adultery' influenced the inclusion of the victim's sexual history in the evidence, even though this inclusion was an infringement of her constitutional rights (2014: 164). Other countries in Africa have also embraced and integrated conservative religious discourse on sexuality within their laws as a means of enforcing what 'conservative religious fundamentalists' (2014: 156) refer to as defending morality. Cited in Tamale's argument are Uganda's law against homosexuality, and the erosion of the right of women to have safe abortions in Nigeria.

Sexuality, as Jessica Horn (2006) points out, is and has been the point of definition, control and violation of African women's bodies, where first a colonising and later a modernising agenda have been enforced. African women bear the brunt of this, having to live a respectability based on domesticity that 'reinforce[s] the idea that the "proper" or "real" African woman is a woman who is heterosexual, married, bears children, and more often than not, pleases her husband sexually' (2006: 9). Horn also sees this narrative as furthered by Catholic and Pentecostal arguments about what is 'biblically correct' being taken up in support of what is 'culturally correct' according to the African leaders who decide on legislation. Horn writes about the need for the sexual rights of women to be recognised and uplifted.

In her chapter, 'Researching and Theorising Sexualities in Africa', in *African Sexualities*, Tamale (2011) echoes this 'rights' discourse. She also expresses a need for attending to the nuances of African sexuality in research. Foregrounding the exotically African body is as vicious as keeping research on African sexualities within the safe boundaries of health and violence. Sexualities are to be discussed as African stories told by Africans in their own terms: stories of pleasure, rights, desires, agency and so forth. They are to be stories told responsibly and ethically, by moving away from the stereotypes promoted by centuries of colonial and Western thought on what Africa is and what Africans represent. Our stories are also to represent a plurality of sexualities without shying away from the intricate and vital links between sexuality and gender. These links continue to inform, after all, the power relations and dynamics within our continent.

The relationship between sexuality and gender affects the choices of those who conform to the laws of respectability, and has consequences for those who choose to defy and challenge these laws. As Chipo Hungwe (2006) outlines, these laws are never static but change over time and with circumstances. Hungwe reviews the transition of the binary 'respectable' versus 'unrespectable' definitions of femininity from colonial times in Southern Africa through to the present. At each historical point, the changes to what is considered respectable have been made to serve patriarchal agendas, and result in the gaining and loss of respectability by certain women. A respectable woman is given a certain level of 'honour', whereas the unrespectable woman is seen as a deviant and labelled a 'prostitute' by society – be it in urban or rural settings and in politics, academia or the home. My discussion about respectable dress codes with Pentecostal women shows how, as in Hungwe's study, the use of the term 'prostitute' is a signifier of 'othered' women who are undeserving of a respectable status.

Tamale (2016) questions the laws of a respectable sexuality and womanhood in an article on the Ugandan 'miniskirt law', by speaking of the eroticising of the female body through the control of dress: 'ironically, the law that was passed ostensibly to protect women from violence was fuelling it. It emboldened Ugandans to abuse women's rights. The already appropriated feminine body was turned into a site for further socio-political contestation' (2016: 86–87).

Evelyn Lutwama-Rukundo (2016) contends that it is fear that fuels and justifies these moral codes. Male and female moralists fear that 'skimpy clothes will unleash female sexuality and free the female body from the tight clutches of patriarchy' (2016: 55). Yet, even within the crippling confines of a closely guarded morality, African women such as Sheeba Karungi – the subject of Lutwana-Rukundo's article – continue to dress in 'skimpy attire' as a means of asserting their agency. Sheeba is a Ugandan musician and performer whose performances and public appearances are highly sexualised and eroticised. Lutwama-Rukundo associates Sheeba's sexual confidence with her agency as a woman, and argues that Sheeba's style of music and dress is an engagement in 'explicit sexual advocacy' (2016: 58).

Whether African women are conforming to or resisting the moralistic codes placed on their beauty and fashion, their bodies are always a site of cultural, religious and legal contention. African women's sexual choices and their bodiness are highly socialised and conditioned (Dosekun 2016). How women see themselves is always in relation to how others may see them. Beauty, respectability and fashion are fitted into discourses that always call women's agency into question, and that keep women's bodies as the colony of gendered discourses. Freeing African women's bodies from this gendered colonisation requires what Pumla Dineo Gqola calls a 'historicized feminist undoing' (2007: 111).

Colonisation and apartheid sewed violence into the fabric of South African society, and the patriarchal structure of both Black and white communities had this violence and militarisation played out on gendered lines. These are problems that continue to haunt us. Gqola notes the dangers of power relations reproduced by gendered discourse, which 'in the South African public sphere are very conservative in the main: they speak of "women's empowerment" in ways that are not transformative, and as a consequence, they exist very comfortably alongside overwhelming evidence that South African women are not empowered' (2007: 115). These discourses force Black South African women into a 'cult of femininity' (2007: 116) that ensures that even the select few chosen for positions of economic and political power adapt to the current structural systems rather than transform them. The 'cult of femininity' also keeps South Africa's violent culture and structure of power in place to silence abused women, keep women in compliance with a patriarchal and homophobic system, and have women limit their movements in an attempt to protect themselves from gender-based violence.

Gender-based violence has been elevated to a culture. It is being made into a state of normality by its repeated occurrence, and has been backgrounded to build and reproduce the 'female fear factory' (Gqola 2017a: 76–137). This constant and repeated action ensures that fear is manufactured in mass form, rendering all women – those who will be or are already victims, and all those who wish to interrupt this cycle of violence – vulnerable to its dangers. The 'female fear factory' presents itself as rape, the shaming of sexuality and fashion choices, and all forms of policing women and vulnerable others.

It is through addressing this physical, cultural and spiritual control that we can bring in a discussion of embodiment and its fleshing out, by recontextualising Hortense J. Spillers' (1987) theorisation of the flesh. Spillers argues that the enslavement of Africans moved the diasporic body from gendered to colour lines. Black women became both invisible and hypervisible: they were as captive as Black men, owned by white men, and subjected to physical, sexual and social tortures. Spillers goes on to argue that slavery dragged the captive through degrees of reduction: from being a thing for the captor to a physical other, and finally, to an embodiment 'that slides into a more general "powerlessness," resonating through various centers of human and social meaning' (1987: 67). This leads her to distinguish between body and flesh to mark the difference between the free and the captive. She defines the very act of capture, the torture and pain that is enacted in the capturing, as one that is done to the *flesh* of the Black body.

Gqola's 'fear factory' brings this torture and pain of the 'female' flesh into our current context. Considering the 'fear factory' as a matter of ownership and the 'female' as the occupied body – Spillers' 'captive' – this body 'focuses a private and particular space, at which point of convergence biological, sexual, social, cultural, linguistic, ritualistic, and psychological fortunes join' (Spillers 1987: 67). The control of flesh through policing, rape and shaming is one I also read as being done to Black women's flesh through discourses and actions that dismember the physical from the social, cultural and spiritual. Tsitsi Dangarembga gives the same reading of the flesh in the Zimbabwean colonial context of her novel *The Book of Not* (2006).

In the novel, Sister Emmanuel calls Tambu and her African dormitory mates in to reassure them that the new government quotas will not affect their places at the school. She says, 'whatever memoranda they send us, we aren't going to chop anyone in half, nor in any other portion' (Dangarembga 2006: 73). The words are a crude joke in response to which the girls 'giggle'. But Tambu is also angered by these words, and wonders how and why Sister Emmanuel sees fit to '[talk] to us like that, making jokes about our flesh and how some people thought it was divisible. Or else it was all lumped as one: your flesh fractioned or piled together!' (2006: 74).

Tambu is a young woman who has the realisation that her body is not her own: that her flesh is owned enough by a colonial government and school to be divided into quotas; that hers is a flesh that must live in fear, dismembered from freedom, and at the mercy of those who can choose to protect it or divide it. The flesh of the girls in *The Book of Not* is an illustration of dismemberment. The girls are physically dismembered from themselves – when cut in half or other portions – and within their race and gender classification – when all are lumped together as one – and they are also socially dismembered from their bodies.

When the Black woman's flesh is considered a site for and of the captor, then the violence that is enacted on it is violence justified. The flesh can be torn apart by rape, torture, shaming and policing. The flesh can also be lumped together into one undifferentiated Black woman, with a universal experience of pain. This is so when anthropology ignores or sensationalises Black women. The Black woman's flesh can be portioned into whatever parts the captor sees fit, when this undifferentiated body falls at the mercy of interpretation by those who do not (will not) see the interiority of Black women's lives. And this pain reconverges into a sociality of powerlessness that is produced and reproduced in many forms.

Similar to the 'female fear factory', and (re)produced within religious circles, is the 'unholy trinity', a term coined by Sorojini Nadar (2005a). Nadar (2005a, 2005b) studies the Indian Pentecostal community in South Africa and makes a similar contention about gender, culture and morality to Tamale (2014). Nadar makes a link between Christianity and moralistic demands to 'return' to culture, and sees an alliance between culture, religion and social constructions of gender working for the constant oppression of women, which she terms the 'unholy trinity' (2005b). The 'unholy trinity' cements the superiority of men over women, and has society believing that this placing is established and unchangeable. Nadar argues that 'women (and men) cannot simply opt out of religion and culture' (2005b: 20). Even those who do opt out do not necessarily escape the violent consequences of these beliefs. It is counterstrategies by those who subscribe to religion that Nadar suggests should be employed within religious communities. These counterstrategies should use religion – she focuses on Christianity in particular – as a tool to undo the oppression of women. Nadar (2005a) takes the role of the spirit in Pentecostal interpretations of the Bible as one such counterstrategy. The spirit does not hold women to patriarchal practices, so the spirit's importance in Pentecostalism should not be undermined. Instead, we should employ a framework that understands the spirit as multifaceted and aiding in the liberation and empowerment of women (Gabaitse 2015).

The intersections between culture, religion and the law are also evident in the discourses I research and in the narratives of the women with whom I converse. Speaking to these women uncovers how they relate to the discourses of their churches, and in turn relate their contexts and experiences to these discourses. These women also place great importance on their relationship with spirituality. It is not so much their agency in interacting with the discourses of their churches that is in question, but how these interactions affect both their social and spiritual lives – their flesh and bodies. This book uncovers these women's identities in relation to their views on gendered roles, moral codes and spirituality. I also consider how these roles, codes and views are internalised by Charismatic women, and interplay and enter into conflict with institutional and class systems to drive their behaviour and choices.

Women's power, then, where the embodied Pentecostal Black woman is concerned, is an attempt to re-member the flesh into a liberated body.

Gender as performativity

Butler (1988, 1990) speaks of 'performativity' to describe the acts and actions that inform and maintain gender identities. She argues that on one level is the awaiting of an authority to prescribe what it is to be, and the building up of that very prescription in anticipation of it. We create the phenomenon of gender as though it were external, when in fact every action we take in anticipation of a gender prescription is the very production of gender. On the next level is our repeated practice, our 'doing' and ritualising gender that gives it a 'naturalised' state through our embodiments (Butler 1990). This performativity does not only happen within and for ourselves, but through an existing frame that we know and see through the discourses and actions of those before and amongst us. We perform for ourselves and we perform out of a desire to receive recognition. We see ourselves to have achieved 'being human', and properly so, when our performance allows us its socially recognisable normality. Gender performativity, according to Butler, is a field of struggles.

To be a woman 'is to have *become* a woman, to compel the body to conform to an historical idea of "woman", to induce the body to become a cultural sign, to materialise oneself in obedience to an historically delimited possibility, and to do this as a sustained and repeated corporeal project' (Butler 1988: 522, emphasis in the original). This material self manifests in differing ways. The construction of femininity is never complete because it 'becomes a productive, embodied constituting of the self' (Mupotsa 2015b: 191). Butler uses the word 'strategy' to account for the pressures under which performing gender takes place. I will use Danai Mupotsa's study of 'white weddings' in Southern Africa as an example of such a strategy, where marriage rites are one way in which femininity can be strategically re/produced (Mupotsa 2014, 2015a, 2015b).

The Black bride presents herself through wedding rituals, dress and photography in a personhood opposing the popular discourse of gendered and racialised other. The white wedding is a way of controlling her body by prescribing whiteness as the racial norm or ideal. Whiteness also controls sexuality because it represents purity. Mupotsa contends that the achievement of femininity requires heterosexuality and work towards beauty.

Comparing heterosexuality to drag, Butler (1993) suggests that they are similar in their imitation of gender. Where drag is an obvious or even exaggerated form of imitation, it is no different from heterosexuality, which constantly imitates and reproduces itself to maintain the status of originality and respectability. Drag, like the white weddings Mupotsa studies, is not an idealisation of the original in heterosexual gender forms, because heterosexuality correspondingly aims to imitate an idealisation of itself. Like drag and the wedding, heterosexuality needs constant repetition to reach a completeness it can never attain in its efforts to claim originality and respectability. Yet, unlike the white wedding, drag exposes the anxieties of the heterosexual claim to normality by foregrounding what the respectable gender tries to exclude. But heterosexual and white normalities expose themselves through the white wedding as the not quite stable, never complete desire for the proper, to which Mupotsa draws our attention. In her conclusion, Mupotsa calls out the failures of this strategy of the proper human as 'not simply failure' but a critique that exposes and makes fragile that which respectability tries to exclude (2014: 270).

Christian women perform this materialisation as they enter the Pentecostal space in obedience, or a negotiation thereof. Their femininities are in process and a project that may be of their choosing, but the choices are given by the discourses and practices of the churches in which they congregate: what Charismatic women foreground in their performance and re/production of a respectable femininity and what they exclude are two of the questions I try to answer in this book. I observe and converse with Charismatic Christian women to come to an understanding of their performativity, desire and interaction with the discourses of their respective churches. I also examine the roles, attitudes and stereotypes within Charismatic discourses that aim to build the gender identities of these women congregants. Yet, finding the answers to the questions of femininity and of the fragility of heterosexuality is not only dependent on recognising the existence of gender performativity but also requires bringing to the fore women's voices, even when they whisper.

Wilful whispers

> *Ko kerekeng* [At church], what's good for me
> *ingena la* [goes in through this ear] but what I don't
> like *iphuma la* [goes out through the other].
> — Lerato, a 28-year-old procurement
> buyer, mother of three

Mupotsa speaks of the self-presentation of Black African women as brides, and Butler of the strategies of performing gender in order to gain recognition. Both bring to our attention a sense of agency, and the pressures that expose but also attempt to disguise the instability of gender. To define femininities as both power and failure, as proper but incomplete, and as choice but also obedience, as hypervisible in flesh but embodied in invisibility, makes the situation of women a paradoxical one. If paradox is to be understood as lacking in logic, or as the absurd, then all who are defined or identify as women become the illustration of absurdity.

Bhuvaneswari's suicide is the subject of Gayatri Chakravorty Spivak's interrogation of feminine absurdity in her famous essay 'Can the Subaltern Speak?' (Spivak 1988). Hers is the story of a tragedy that could have easily been written off as a failure of respectability but for the timing of her suicide – Bhuvaneswari took her own life while menstruating, proof that she was not pregnant and therefore not attempting to escape the shame of an illicit pregnancy. It was later found out that she was a member of a group fighting for the independence of India, tasked to assassinate but choosing rather to die. Hence the absurdity of a young woman proving respectability by disrespecting the 'privilege' of a *sati* suicide. This type of suicide was a sacrifice of widows, practised historically by Hindus in South Asia, where the widow was placed on her husband's funeral pyre. The act was considered one of heroic sacrifice by a devoted wife. How absurd to die by one's own hand – agentic and wilful – to escape a task, but also to be remembered by family and comrades as loyal to the cause for independence, faithful to a husband she was yet to have, and respectful towards her culture. Bhuvaneswari becomes a representation of absurdity. Hers is a story of an incomplete life: a young woman who fights to die in a body considered pure and kept for proper relations with a husband, but impure because she bleeds. Absurd that a woman's cycle is both impure and proof of purity. Absurd that a woman who makes such a bold statement is voiceless.

In rewriting the story of Bhuvaneswari's suicide, Spivak invites us to listen closely to her wilful whisper. I see this story, and the question 'can the subaltern speak?' as a necessary reminder for us to listen to, rather than take part in the epistemological quest to colonise, the subaltern body. For in between our necessary feminist pursuits to question the institutions that define gender in the name of patriarchy are the whispers of those we stand and fight for. These whispers are a negotiation of resistance and recognition. And if we are to listen carefully to the tone of Lerato's words quoted in the epigraph to this section – her chosen silence in resistance – we can employ an analysis that Nthabiseng Motsemme (2004a, 2004b) invites us to use in reading, understanding and giving necessary recognition to silence as language. Motsemme's analysis of silence allows us to platform subaltern 'muteness' as voice for coping with, and also reinventing, 'the unjust world they daily occup[y]' (2004b: 5).

Reading the question of desire closely also means listening to the cultural politics of emotion. I borrow Sara Ahmed's (2014a) phrasing here to read bodies as being shaped by contact with others and to connect agency with will: will 'as a condition of possibility for human freedom' as well as a 'moral faculty' (Ahmed 2014b: 60). It is in reading will as a pursuit of good that I hear and observe Charismatic women's voices, and their attempts at bending even the wills and the desires they consider to be out of *their* bounds of morality. I read their wilful desires for freedom, and happiness, within the cracks between complying with hegemony and asserting difference. Listening closely can redefine the paradox of Black African femininity as not absurd but rather conflicted in the yearning for freedom.

Conclusion

I began this chapter by problematising not only how pain is used to universalise the Black feminised other but also the tendency to employ pain as the only Black African feminine experience. Exposing how religion, culture and the law employ gendered discourses to sustain constraining patriarchal systems is important, as it uncovers the roots of this pain. But it is equally important to do also what Tamale asks of Blackwomen researchers: to nuance Black women's sexuality beyond health, oppression and pain. This nuance brings us into conversation with the identities women create for themselves to resist or conform to the laws of sexuality. Nuancing experiences also requires our digging into the histories that build these experiences, so that we can enter into an analysis of the Black African feminine body as a colonial site.

Behaviour and choices, then, are more than just what Black women do and have. They are an unstable place, a struggle for recognition, and a strategy of self-constituting and re-membrance. The performative is both production and seeking. Hence Mupotsa's contention that femininities are never complete. I draw a paradox from this reading of incompleteness within recognition. Theories of performativity and becoming raise questions about Pentecostal women that are more nuanced than the conclusions of most studies of African Pentecostal women by white scholars: 'Pentecostal women are [fill in the gap]'. My knowledge of the Pentecostal Charismatic women of Alexandra as incomplete, struggling, flourishing, wilful, obedient, silent, resistant, all at the same time, is the starting point of my finding their voices, even when they crack, and even when they whisper.

So, in this chapter I have sought to use Blackwomen theory to redefine Black women's voices and power: not because giving voice back to the women with whom I converse is solely in my and other Blackwomen theorists' hands, but because I am ever more convinced of the importance of Blackwomen theoretical frameworks as a necessity for the foregrounding of Black women's experiences. It is out of this necessity that I enter the cracks between the Black feminised other and Black women's power.

Chapter 4

This field I call home

Obatla ho ngwala karona [she wants to write about us], and she's one of us. Don't you want your story to be known?
— Sheila, 34-year-old personal assistant

In September 2019, a talk based on my research on Pentecostal constructions of femininity in Alexandra township, titled 'Theorising from the Epicentres of Our Agency', was included in the African Feminisms (Afems) annual conference at the University of the Witwatersrand, in Johannesburg. My celebration of having an abstract accepted was to be topped with having my name on the programme under the theme 'Inside Outsider/Outside Insider'. Colleagues 'got' me, understood my positionality from reading just 200 words of an abstract, and no one was confused by what it is that I am trying to do.

A few months prior to this, I was asked to speak at the University of Johannesburg's School of Communication annual Research Bootcamp about my experiences 'in the field'. My initial response was that I could not talk about the field because I do not work in one. My research is based at home. The reason I decided to start a research project on Pentecostal constructions of femininity was because it is personal. I grew up in church, and I know Charismatic Christianity as well as I know myself: well enough to know that a lot of questions about womanhood, and my womanhood too, have not been answered to my satisfaction. I had to know if there might be other women who are made as uncomfortable as I am by some of the Pentecostal discourses that aim to fashion our becoming women. If the answer was yes, then I had to know why they keep going to church, as I keep going.

It had not occurred to me at the time I began to ask these questions aloud that I would have to align myself with mostly white anthropologists and ethnographers who visit and write about Charismatic churches in Africa, coming from social, cultural, linguistic and religious backgrounds different from their research grounds and participants. They are in the field; I am at home. The study of African Pentecostal Charismatic Christianity comprises mostly anthropological views of the African churchgoer that, with the exception of scholars like Allan Anderson (2002, 2013, 2018) and a few others (see Burchardt 2018; Mate 2002; Schenectady & Parsitau 2017), have focused on the 'Americanised' megachurches.[9] These views often narrowly identify the Charismatic movement with the prosperity gospel.

I was finally convinced that my home field is an important vantage point because, while work done by scholars such as Deborah James (2019) and Maria Frahm-Arp (2015b, 2016) has added a more nuanced scholarly view of Pentecostal Charismatic Christianity in Africa and the global south, what is missing is writing by Black women such as myself who are part of the Pentecostal community and are an embodied voice within the movement, rather than a mere object of research. And though I include reference to the sensitive and embodied anthropologies of Judith Casselberry and Elizabeth Pritchard (2019) in the first chapter of this book, it is still my view that megachurches and celebrity Pentecostalisms are given more attention than the smaller, communal churches on which my study is based. In this way, I pay heed to Michel-Rolph Trouillot's argument for ethnographies 'that offer new points of reentry by questioning the symbolic world upon which "nativeness" is premised' and 'that aim explicitly at the destabilization and eventual destruction of the Savage slot' (Trouillot 2003: 22).

My positioning as a Black woman within the Pentecostal movement belongs to the genre of (auto)ethnographies that Cheryl Rodriguez (2001) describes in 'A Homegirl Goes Home', where she asserts the importance of Black feminist scholarly interventions from members of communities, but also delves into the problems one can simultaneously encounter and create both for oneself and the community one studies as a 'native' scholar. Nikki Lane also underscores the importance of reflexivity in ethnographic studies 'because the ethnographer must constantly consider how her body is *affecting* and is *effected* by the communities and institutions in which she is embedded' (2016: 632, emphasis in the original). So, taking on the role of 'auto' in ethnography makes me aware of issues of positionality. Positionality has, in fact, been a point of debate within race studies (see, for instance, Milner IV [2007]), feminist scholarship (see, for instance, Harding [2004]), and religious studies (see McCutcheon [1999]). Although aware of these broader debates, I am entering them as a Black feminist (auto)ethnographer from the specific vantage point of African Pentecostal scholarship as the field in which my book intervenes.

This chapter seeks to answer the critical question of how I have come to know what I know, and what I present as meaningful knowledge of Pentecostal women in Alexandra and their femininity. I also take this chapter as an opportunity to write my entry into the field I call home, my subjectivity, reflexivity, subject position and the vignettes I flow into and out of as an (auto)ethnographer of/with my community. And I begin this writing with the knowledge and acknowledgement that I do not walk this home ground alone, nor am I the first to be an insider/ outsider. I follow in the footsteps and stand on the shoulders of mothers and sisters who have theorised and documented the importance of writing our own stories, and worked tirelessly and sometimes thanklessly to hone an epistemological space where my identity as a Black woman, native to the community I study, and my role as a researcher are not three conflicting identities from which I am compelled to choose. They are instead 'a seminal point of departure for our theorization and simultaneously…a point of entry for our ethnographic research' (McClaurin 2001: 16). Many are these women, but I will name just three of them and their work. Danai Mupotsa, whose extensive studies of weddings, including traditional rituals leading up to white weddings, include her own experiences as (becoming) an African bride (2014, 2015a, 2015b).[10] Sarojini Nadar, who waives the claim to objective neutrality in her womanist critique of the Full Gospel Church of God in Southern Africa (2005a), where she was a member for 18 years. Finally, Cynthia B. Dillard, who has written an autobiographical account of her experiences as an administrator at a white university alongside other Black women's experiences to articulate an 'endarkened feminist epistemology' that 'disrupts the idea of neutral relationships and structures in inquiry and points instead to the complex nature of research when it maintains allegiance and substantive connections to the very communities under study' (2000: 662).

I introduced this book by writing about the importance of Black women's experiences as a foregrounded knowledge base, and about my dedication to documenting and bringing the flesh to Blackwomen theory. This 'fleshiness' of the experience of these women requires one to spend extended periods of time with them, engaging their knowledge by observing and talking with them, and exploring their values, practices and sense of identity (Hodgson 2001; Lane 2016). My life has been spent doing just that, but only during the past few years as a researcher who values (auto)ethnography as a Black (African) feminist/womanist methodology (Brown-Vincent 2019).

I selected the churches where I would conduct research through my familial network, as my mother is a pastor in Alexandra (figure 4.2). The first choice was an easy one. Bishop Silawuli is a good friend of my mother and visits often for prayer and Bible readings at my home. He was happy to have me record his sermons for research, especially knowing that it would not be yet another criticism of the collection of tithes. It was my asking to speak to the women at his church that complicated things a little. Bishop Silawuli seemed uncomfortable with the idea and suggested that I have my 'talks' with an elder present – preferably his wife, Pastor Silawuli. I was prepared for this hitch, knowing that the Charismatic churches I go to tend to be suspicious of young(er) single women being alone without the supervision of a more experienced and married woman. I also knew that there would be some suspicion about my intentions with the women, since I have never hidden my feminist stance from any of my mother's friends. These are elements about me that push me to the outer limits of the hierarchical 'charmed circle' of sexuality (see Rubin 1984; Tamale 2011). They call into question, in Pentecostal pastors' reasoning, what kind of influence I would have on women congregants, sitting and conversing alone with them. This awareness of my position as a feminist, and how it can (however well-meaning and meant to empower my community) become a site of conflict with that very community, also serves to inform my experiences as an (auto)ethnographer and my approach to the people I aim to foreground in my research. Being a feminist in a Black community, and especially a religious one, 'continues to be misrepresented, distorted, or dismissed as though being both Black and feminist are two mutually exclusive and/or conflicting experiences' (Rodriguez 2001: 238).

I had to assure Bishop Silawuli that my intention was not so much to 'talk to them' as to have them 'talk to me', so my own opinions and lifestyle would not be imposed on the women. I wanted to give them a chance to talk about their lives in church, how the sermons they listen to affect them, and how, when or if they apply what they learn in church elsewhere. Once I had told him this, the pastor started to relax. I then added that my fear about having an 'elder' in the room while I had conversations with the women congregants was that they would feel pressurised to speak only in a way that felt acceptable to the church: I would not get their full and honest stories. This he understood very well, agreeing and adding that maybe the women do need to speak to someone other than his wife or other elders. His exact words were '*ingabhakhulula lenxokolo*' ['this talk might set them free'], plus, he smiled, '*ungumntwana womfundisi, kufana nokuba ungumfundisi nawe*' ['you are a pastor's child, so you may as well be a pastor yourself']. This initial interaction with Bishop Silawuli was to inform how I approached the other pastors. With them, I made sure to put myself forward as first a responsible pastor's child and only then a researcher.

My mother's position as a pastor did well to carry me out of the outskirts and into the Pentecostal charmed circle and, in the words of Layli Phillips and Barbara McCaskill, I was 'able to reformulate these disparate yet fundamental elements of my existence in terms of complementarity rather than tension and to realize that both could be harmonized without the sacrifice of either' (2006: 87).

These words are shared by Phillips and McCaskill to describe the marrying of their Black woman and researcher identities, yet they fit so well as an illustration of the intergenerational relations I have with my mother, her colleagues (the pastors) and their female congregants (my participants), and how they are an integral dimension of knowledge production concerning African feminisms. I am a researcher, a member of the community, a Blackwoman theorist, and a daughter who needed my mother's assistance to break through the barriers of a gendered and age-based religiosity. I am all these identities that serve to complement each other, as long as I choose not to see them as tensions; and as long as I am open to conversations (such as the one with Bishop Silawuli) that lead us to an understanding which places me as one who can be trusted. So, although I first pointed out my charmed circle limitations, it is the recognition of our intergenerational relationality and understanding that closes that gap. My mother being a pastor brings me closer to being a researcher amongst pastors, a feminist amongst Black women congregants, and as good as a pastor within my Pentecostal charismatic community.

So, establishing rapport with the Pentecostal women I was to speak to was not a difficult task as, in their eyes, I was as good as a pastor. Pastors not only present sermons at church. They serve as counsellors, advice givers and prayer partners. I know this from growing up in a home where people would walk in crying and leave elated, where exhausted women would fall asleep on our couch and wake up to thank my mother for giving them rest like they had never experienced before, and where troubled strangers would knock and ask to speak to 'moruti' ['the pastor'] after being referred by friends, neighbours or family. People in my community trust pastors and, as I learned, their children, by default. This relieved me of the task of having to establish a rapport with my participants, but it meant that I could not take my responsibility towards them lightly.

Getting volunteers from the churches to be participants worked differently at each church. Nkuli, Bishop and Pastor Silawuli's daughter, was my entry point to the women at Upper Hall Ministries. We grew close as children when our parents grouped us together (Nkuli, her sister Bongi, my brother Tebogo and me) for singing at church events and at my grandmother's last birthday party and my sister's wedding. The four of us got along well as children and still do as adults. On the first day I arrived at the church to record Pastor Silawuli's sermon, Nkuli included a reminder in her announcements to the women who had volunteered that they were to set aside time the following week after church for our conversation. Her announcement also included reminding the women who are elders and over the ages I had asked for (20–45) to please excuse themselves from this meeting. Initially, I had planned to cap the age of the women at 45, but two women just over that age (46 and 48) expressed their disappointment at my leaving them out. I moved the age up for them because I could not justify even to myself why their experiences could not be included. The women at Upper Hall brought additional snacks and baked goods to this 'meeting' to add to the snacks I had already offered to provide.

At large church services, where more than one church gathers, food is usually provided at the end of the service for all who attend. This is a tradition I have known since childhood, and I always look forward to the laughter and conversations at these lunches (figure 4.1). I know from experience that people relax and are willing to chart the conversational territory of their personal lives outside of church. This is a time when I have seen different sides of women who are willing to talk 'dirty' and occasionally joke about putting their Bibles aside to address secular matters. Mupotsa (2020) notes the value of narratives at the 'kitchen tea parties', where the presence of food (and in her case alcohol) shared amongst women creates an atmosphere where 'secret' pleasures, memories and desires are shared. My provision of food when meeting with the women after their church services was a means to recreate that atmosphere. I also provided food because Charismatic church services can be long (up to three hours or more depending on the type of service) and I did not want to risk losing valuable narratives because the women were hungry and tired. My participants also volunteered to add to the food I provided. In this sharing of time and nutrition I read a feminist ethics of care. Like Neo Sinoxolo Musangi (2018), I choose to see the relations between women, specifically the women who participate in my research and whom I write about, as ones of care – not as 'a value project or a legal battleground' but rather as a 'network of ethical being(s)' (2018: 410). Care work speaks to femininities and to feminism as a relational point through which divisive distinctions, and in my case the distinctions between the researcher and the researched, can begin to dissolve.

At Living Waters, Rose Nyathi introduced me to her congregation, as a pastor's daughter who could be trusted, just before the church service ended. She asked me to stand in front of all of them and tell them my plans. A crowd of bright faces looked up at me standing in front of the pulpit, eagerly waiting to hear my message. I think they thought I would be delivering a sermon or inviting them to a special service at my own church. But news that I was conducting research for my academic project did not disappoint them. Thankfully, it seemed to make them even more eager to listen. At the end of the service, three women came to give me their cellphone numbers and to tell me that they could not wait to be a part of my project. The first to volunteer, Sheila, gave me her details quickly and then stopped two other women at the gate as they were about to leave. She convinced them of the importance of 'our' stories being documented. They then came over to give me their names and phone numbers too. So I had five women from Living Waters, and then the number went up to six the following week when our session was about to begin. It was Nancy who approached me as we were setting up our lunch and seats, telling me that she had not been at church the week before but had heard about my project from the others and wanted her story included too. I was more than happy to add one more voice to the group.

At Red Sea Ministries and God's Love, the two women pastors gave my cellphone number to the women at their churches. Four women from God's Love and five from Red Sea Ministries sent me WhatsApp texts expressing their interest and offering to add what they could to the snacks I would be providing.

Looking back at these interactions and how I came to gain participants in my research uncovers an important realisation about these women. That is, the women who volunteered to talk with me are not only sources of knowledge production (see Collins 2000; Dillard 2000), but are also well aware of how they are represented by people outside their communities, including in the media, and that motivated them to take part in the telling of our own stories. Sheila's convincing of some of the women to participate, and my being approached by others who had initially been left out by my age requirements, shows how the women themselves see the importance of sharing their experiences out of a politics of necessity. In other words, all of the women who volunteered their experiences stand willing to be the 'natives' who talk and gaze back (Jacobs-Huey 2002). The women offered their voices, and I have used them 'to transform the anthropological canon so that it reflects the richness and validity of Black feminist thought' (Rodriguez 2001: 236).

My initial raw data consisted of eight sermons of approximately one hour each, one poem recited by a lay pastor from Upper Hall, and two short sermons delivered at a wedding-announcement ceremony at Red Sea Ministries. All these sermons are recorded. I also employed field notes as an 'analysis in vivo' (Gibson & Brown 2009: 105), where the notes do not necessarily record a series of events but serve as a reminder of subjects that stood out for me while listening to the sermons. These ideas were then taken forward in my discussions with the women congregants, and then in the organising and analysis of the data.

Attending at least two services at each church gave me a chance to observe the women with whom I would be conversing. I noted their dress styles and body language during the services and sermons, and the way they related to each other in church, at the end of the services and when we all sat down to speak. All of this became part of the data that I present and interpret in the ethnographic chapter to follow.

Because I had all the women's phone numbers and they had saved mine too, I was able to view their WhatsApp stories and get more insight into their lives, values and beliefs. Since WhatsApp was bought by Facebook in 2014, users are able to post 'stories' similar to those on Facebook to share their lives with close contacts. Unlike Facebook, where one receives and sends 'friend requests', or follows and likes the pages and posts of 'friends', WhatsApp provides intimacy in sharing as only those who are in one's phone contacts are able to view the stories posted. Also, unlike Facebook, the stories posted by users are only available for 24 hours. WhatsApp is not only easily accessible, but as I have said, provides a sense of social intimacy and a sociality of dwelling (O'Hara et al. 2014). This has allowed me to keep close contact with all of the women without always seeing them. At the end of our sessions many of the women asked that we do this more often, as they had enjoyed speaking so freely with me. This is also how I received their permission to view their WhatsApp posts. I am still in contact with some of them, sharing jokes and catching up on stories we shared. Seven of the women also invited me to their homes or came to my home to tell me more stories that they did not have time to share within the group. All of this, plus the approximately two-hour-long group conversations at each church, meant that I had a lot of data in my hands.

The truth is, I do not consider myself to be 'like a pastor' in the least. But this assigned identity became my entry point into this ethnographic research. It was my insider status that afforded me the ease of access to my research participants, and the effortless way in which our conversations flowed. In the chapter to follow I mention a few occurrences where the women took my being a pastor's daughter as their way of relaying messages about their unhappiness with some of the leadership of their churches and their handling of matters. Some women would tell me of a grievance with the church and ask me to write it down and make sure I told 'them' (the pastors). I know from this positionality that nothing about our conversations and their allowing me into their social media lives and homes can be taken for granted. Being 'like a pastor' held a subjective power other than placing me in the circle with these women. This assigned identity also placed me in danger of falling into a similar set-up to my counterparts in the academic field of Pentecostalism studies. Researchers like Frahm-Arp (2012, 2015a) and Van Wyk (2014) – who are amongst the most prominent scholars in this field in South Africa – are most likely writing up the performances their informants put on for them, as participants often give a side of themselves and their stories that they believe the ethnographer wants to see or hear (Zinn 1979). Being 'like a pastor', native as I am, could place me in the same position, except that the women with whom I speak think that I want to hear how well versed they are in the Bible.

Therefore, I applied an 'interview technique' similar to the semi-/unstructured interviewing that Mupotsa (2011) uses to allow her interviewees to lead their conversations. Mupotsa proposes a method that goes beyond writing oneself into one's research and has the specific aim of placing oneself in an 'object' position. She navigates the sensitivity of her subject area in this way as a means to share her own experiences, in order to open up a space for her participants to feel comfortable sharing their experiences. She makes two contentions in her choice of this interview technique: firstly, that its informality 'allows for a reciprocal relationship to foster between the [interviewer and interviewee] as the interview can take the shape of a conversation'; and secondly, that it enacts an ethic of listening carefully, so that the researcher does not only hear answers to specific questions but follows 'the direction that the women [she speaks] to take [her] in' (Mupotsa 2011: 101–102).

I too wanted to ensure that the conversations I had with Pentecostal women were led by them and highlighted issues important to them. The technique I applied, hoping to get similar results to those of Mupotsa, is one I took from my mother, who uses it when counselling people as a pastor. My mother taught me that being a pastor means allowing people to speak in 'stages' that lead to their being comfortable with sharing their story. The first of these stages happens in the first 15 to 30 minutes of a conversation and is what she calls 'Bible Olympics'. This is when the person speaking to a pastor wants to establish themselves as a good Christian, with a deep knowledge of the Bible. The next stage is like the first, in that the interviewee will tell of all the work they have done in the church or about their spiritual gifts, and may possibly include some negative encounters they have had with other pastors or Christians who misunderstood them. This does not last as long as the Bible Olympics stage, and is used by the interviewee/counselee to read the face, expressions and reactions of the pastor. Any negativity they sense from the pastor at this stage has them withdrawing and no longer being willing to speak, because they are afraid of being 'ousted' or judged. My mother suggests that at this stage one should portray a neutral stance but also a willingness to listen further. She would joke with me when I was younger that I could never counsel people because every one of my thoughts could always be read in my eyes. I am an expressive person, but I think I applied the neutral expression well enough on these occasions to get my research participants to the next stage. This is when they trust the pastor/counsellor/interviewer enough to open up about their lives and experiences. But, my mother warns, they will always do a quick scan to read any judgement they think you will have, and it is important that they know that you are always on their side, understanding and willing to learn and know more.

The interviews I had with my participants tested my pastor/ object position. They pushed the insider/outsider space I occupy to the point where the participants in my research project turned their gaze on me and I became the 'subject' of the conversation. The section in the following chapter on desire gives an illustration of how Black feminist (auto)ethnographic work subverts and reinscribes the subject/object relation of researcher and researched.

Another key element of the Black feminist (auto)ethnographic methodology I am presenting is the transcribing and translation of the data collected during the fieldwork. In my own research project this also called on my self-reflexivity as a 'native' researcher. The sermons were not all focused on the topic of gender roles, gender hierarchies or femininities, which meant that I had to select specific instances where these issues were mentioned. My transcripts were therefore a 're-presentation and rendering of data into new form' (Gibson & Brown 2009: 123). This problematised the critical reflexivity I adopted as an ethnographer, as the gaze through which I looked at the language of the church not only determined the way in which I chose the 'important' data from the sermons but also constituted the language in which I chose for the data to take form in my account (Davies, Browne & Petersen 2004; Roberts 1997).

Julia Bailey (2008) argues for the inevitable writing of transcripts to fit the research questions and methodological assumptions of the researcher. It served my research best to focus on gender issues, but using a process of self-reflexivity helped avoid a possible misrepresentation of the sermons (Hodgson 2001; Jones, Adams & Ellis 2016; McClaurin 2001; Owens, Edwards & McArthur 2018). I therefore noted my own opinions, background and hypotheses and presented them with and against the sermons.

My quotations of the pastors' speeches and of the narratives of the women are in the language that they spoke at the time of our conversations. That is, how I write them up in the following chapter is the exact way in which they spoke, including their code-switching between English, Zulu, Xhosa and Tswana. This is done to preserve as much of the speaker's voice as possible, and also preserve the idiolects of Alexandra's unique language culture. I am aware that writing speech acts in this way can be reductionist and patronising to the language user (Davies 2003; Mose Brown & De Casanova 2014). But writing participants' speech in standard English when that is not how they communicate makes the work of translation invisible and unexaminable, and the transcript deceitful to the reader. I give the translations into standard English after the original for those who may not be familiar with local languages. My work of translation does not compare to that of Black feminist ethnographers who have the benefit of citing documented languages such as African American Vernacular English (as do Tamara Mose Brown and Erynn Masi de Casanova [2014]). Nevertheless, I place the language used by Alexandra residents within this research and assert my native ability to translate it as 'crucial to the decolonial turn and to the construction of better "bridging epistemologies" so as to confront the mistranslations or bad translations' (De Lima Costa & Alvarez 2014: 558) that have led to the reductionist representations of African women in Pentecostal research.

This turn is indeed crucial, considering the prevalent academic narratives of Black South African Pentecostal women represented as the sensational and quite likely deranged Phukile (in Van Wyk 2014), or the reductive descriptions of the upwardly mobile 'Romany Cream or Oreo' (in Frahm-Arp 2010). I, for one, do not think of myself, nor do I see the women with whom I congregate, professionals included, in the binary-edible terms of an appetite for whiteness that categorises them as either the black-skinned and white interior of Oreos or the black-skinned and slightly brown interior of Romany Creams. For even when whiteness is an assumed aspiration of Black women, it is important to document Black women's lives in their own words and language to show that there are complexities in their experiences that evidence their autonomy, as opposed to a sole imposition of 'iconic whiteness' (see Simidele Dosekun [2016] on Black beauty).

I analyse the sermons of the pastors using elements of discourse and critical discourse analysis. Both modes of analysis are based on a view of discourse as shared knowledge and ideologies that are produced and reproduced in formal and informal communicative acts (Fairclough 2003; Mama 1995; Tannen,

Hamilton & Schiffrin 2015). The 'critical' in critical discourse analysis points to my aims to uncover the political position taken by an individual or a group, and to understand persistent social issues (Prinsloo 2018; Van Dijk 1993). I am closely examining and uncovering the gender ideology in sermons by Pentecostal ministers. More specifically, my research aims to discover the discursive strategies (Van Dijk 1993) they use to construct femininities and the extent to which these constructions are a concealment or justification of the social order.

Finding the extent of the (re)production of normative gender discourses and ideologies in the construction of femininities involves examining and noting what aspects of femininity are foregrounded or backgrounded in sermons, and identifying processes of transivity where the active or passive voice is used in the pastors' narratives. I also analyse the use of argumentation, which Richardson (2007) bases on categories of rhetorical practice. These are categories that defend or accuse a person; that praise or denunciate; and that focus on future actions that are encouraged if considered to be advantageous or discouraged if they are argued to be disadvantageous.

Where my research participants are concerned, their experiences are the source of knowledge that shows us how, when and to what extent they appropriate or resist and interact with the ideology of these sermons. Therefore, I employ narrative analysis as a means to note, foreground and understand my participants' experiences. Black feminist (auto)ethnography stands as my 'attempt to return to a belief in the power of our productivity informed by a rigorous inquiry into our lived always already intersectional struggles for liberation' (Brown-Vincent 2019: 114), and the reproduction of the narratives of the Pentecostal women in this book is evidence of this power and struggle. Their stories show us the different ways in which they choose to interact with the discourses of their respective churches, and how even in silence they stand in resistance to that which means to oppress them. Further, these women participants volunteered themselves out of an awareness that Black women's experiences have been silenced, oversimplified and misunderstood. It is under these circumstances that their narratives become the voice of resistance (Dillard 2000).

I choose recurring themes expressed by the women at all the churches to show the persistent issues and discourses that they find most important. I use extended quotations to reproduce these accounts, to (re)present these women, to bring forward as much of them and their thoughts and language as is possible given the spatial constraints of this study. This I do based on another contention of Layla Brown-Vincent that Black feminist (auto)ethnography is a means to 'encounter, document, and analyze the stories of Black Women...to make visible that which has been intentionally obscured by white supremacist patriarchal structures and institutions' (2019: 115). Narrative analysis shows not only the identities these women take for themselves, but how they use narratives to 'express and negotiate both individual and collective identities' (De Fina 2015: 351).

My entry into the field I call home gave me a special vantage point in my interactions with the women and pastors of Pentecostal churches in Alexandra. It also gave me the responsibility of not only representing them in academic writing, but also ensuring that this knowledge is a reflection of my critical positionality. And it is because of this assumed position of documenting and analysing through a Black and African feminist lens that I privileged and centred Black women in Pentecostal practice. My 'native' and (auto)ethnographic standing within the community I have studied informed my ethical considerations, analysis and the building of relationships with my participants, as did my use of dialogue not just in the sense of 'formalised' interviews, but as 'conversations'. This choice of methodology not only justifies researching a field of familiarity but brings about a commitment and responsibility to attending to the language, voices and experiences of research participants – in my case the Pentecostal women of Alexandra township – with whom one identifies. The next chapter describes my home ground, and the knowledge I have uncovered within this 'field'.

Figure 4.1. Easter lunch set-up, 2019, hosted by Red Sea Ministries at Thusong Youth Centre.

Source: The author.

Figure 4.2. 'At home' with my mother, singing at a special service.
Source: God's Love Christian Family Church Facebook page, https://
web.facebook.com/Godslovecfc/photos/pb.100064414820623.-
2207520000./8216696238356348/?type=3, accessed 22 October 2022.

Chapter 5

Constructions of femininity

Get me to the church on time

I have never known a time when Sunday and at least one other day of the week have not been set church days. My childhood memories include vivid images of my mother and grandmother in Methodist Church uniforms. My mother as choir lead and my grandmother as a lay minister made sure that we never missed any main or special services. When my parents left the Methodist Church and converted to Pentecostalism, memories of long early morning drives to a church service held in a classroom at a school in Daveyton were imprinted on me. If people were to look for a distinctive structure when trying to find a church, they would be lost to the majority of Charismatic Christian churches in South Africa. Over the past three decades, I have attended services, prayers, special services, all-night prayers, exorcisms, youth conventions and Pastors' Kids (PK) classes in former warehouses, school classrooms, community halls, living rooms, bedrooms, hospitals, tents, garages, prisons, well-built megachurches, stadiums and even open fields.[11] Alexandra – being overpopulated and relatively lacking in space – is no different in the creative ways in which many Charismatic churches have arranged venues to meet on Sundays.

Now join me as I walk, commute and get lifts to four different Charismatic churches in Alexandra at different times, on different Sundays.

After taking a local taxi from my home in 12th Avenue, Alexandra, to 22nd Avenue, I walk up a short, winding road through a block of houses that was originally built for civil servants by the apartheid government.[12] These houses are relatively modern compared to Alexandra's first farm-style houses, with a minimum of three bedrooms, a kitchen and a bathroom. Some have been further renovated, with luxurious-looking walls and lawns that could be mistaken for suburbia, were it not for the buzzing atmosphere of the township.

I have become accustomed to the sounds of different styles of music blaring from people's homes and from cars and taxis driving by. It is a Sunday, so most are playing their favourite R'n'B, jazz or gospel tunes. I pass street vendors selling fruit and vegetables, sweets and cigarettes, and preparing *amagwinya* (fat-cakes) in large pots on a fire (here I hurry to avoid the smell of smoke and fat clinging to my clothes). I walk past women in uniforms rushing to their respective mainline churches, and to *stokvel* meetings. (*Stokvels* are saving schemes, where groups of friends meet to keep each other financially accountable by agreeing on an amount to give each other monthly, in rotation. This tradition was started by women in the early years of Black urban settlement as a means of sending money home to their rural families in bulk, or for building homes or buying furniture [see Matuku & Kaseke 2014; Ngcobo & Chisasa 2018; Verhoef 2001].) I meet boys and men of all ages basking in the sun or enjoying the first cigarette of the day, and I greet them as usual, promising that I will pray for them when I arrive at church – this is a request I have come to expect from many men who believe that church is a 'woman's thing'. I have yet to ask if what they truly believe is that it is a 'woman's service to men'.

Some children are playing on the pavements, others are buying last-minute seven-colour ingredients for the Sunday lunch, and the rest are smartly dressed and walking dutifully with their mothers to church. Following my mother's directions, I keep walking towards London Road and look out for the last driveway on my left before reaching the Zion Christian Church. It is at the end of that driveway that I now see white linen covering a gate. I have arrived at Living Waters Ministries, founded and led by Pastor and Mrs Nyathi. It is now church songs accompanied by handclapping that I hear over the hooting cars and the sounds of the life that goes on just a driveway away. Living Waters Ministries is in the garage and front yard of the Nyathis' home. The chairs are arranged on a turf-like mat in the yard; above them is a large net that has been hooked between the roof and the walls. Most of the chairs have crisp white covers. This is where I take my seat, after being greeted warmly by a middle-aged woman in a grey two-piece dress suit.

I am not sure if the chairs in the front row are reserved for elders, so I take a seat at the far end of the second row to make sure that I am still able to get a good view of the pulpit and the congregants too. I know it is the pulpit I am facing, nestled between the gates we enter through and the seats arranged in the garage to the left. I know this not only because everyone is facing that direction, but also because it is the only thing that is distinctly 'church-like' in this setting. Next to this pulpit is a small table covered with a white tablecloth. On the table sit three baskets marked 'Goodwill Offering', 'Tithe' and 'Special Offering'. Pastor Nyathi and his wife, Rose Nyathi, sit closest to the pulpit, and next to them is an elderly couple. Pastor Nyathi is a stout man, with friendly eyes and a stellar smile. He occasionally wears a tie and jacket, but most days – this one included – he is in a shirt and formal slacks. Rose Nyathi, also called 'Pastor' at times, stands tall by his side in a floral midi-dress and heels.

By the time I have placed my handbag on a chair and joined in the singing and clapping, a few more women have walked in and taken seats or gone into corners to say their prayers. The time is 9:15 a.m. The woman in the grey suit begins and leads another song, after which the entire congregation starts to pray. Every congregant says their own prayer. Some shout and move about, while others kneel and cry quietly, and others still choose to sit with their heads bowed and their lips moving silently. The rest have their hands lifted in the air and faces tilted upwards as if to face the sky. Their eyes are shut. I would usually join in the prayer, but instead choose to say a quick thank you to God for the day and then use the time out to scan the room again. This time I count about 30 adults and teenagers and 15 young children. Two of the women carry small babies on their backs. When this prayer time dies down – with only one or two audible voices remaining – the grey-suited woman begins a new song, which again leads the congregation into prayer. Song–prayer. Song–prayer. It is now 10 a.m.

Ten a.m. on the following Sunday is around the time I begin to make my way to Upper Hall Ministries, led by Bishop and Pastor Silawuli. This time I take a Taxify because I am running late, and the sun is blazing hot. I direct the Taxify driver to 2nd Avenue on Hofmeyr Street where there was once Kings – a budget cinema many of my childhood friends enjoyed for its array of martial arts films. That cinema building has since had many lives, including that of a church, a crèche and now a plumbing warehouse. We cross over the four-way stop street to reach Ko Bareng (The Bar) on the left, where a few people are sitting on chairs and crates at the gate, sipping cold beers. 'You have arrived at your destination,' says the robotic GPS voice, and Sipho the Taxify driver gives me a quizzical look. I think that he cannot imagine what I would be dressed up for to come to a place like this on a Sunday morning, so I offer an explanation: 'There is a church in this yard, in a small room just behind the shebeen.' I then thank him and make my way in.

This is a shebeen yard, so house music and *kwaito* are blaring from the large speakers inside. As I walk past the bar and its patrons, I greet and again dutifully promise to pray for each of them, and they promise to one day join us in church. Upper Hall is in a corrugated iron structure just behind the shebeen. The door is wide open to let some air in, and the first thing I see before walking through it are black plastic chairs sparsely filled by a few women and children – more children than women. They are singing a hymn, '*Uzuliphathe Kahle Ivangeli*' ('Take care of/do not take for granted the Gospel'), and like the church members at Living Waters, are happy to use rhythmic clapping as their only accompanying musical instrument. I join in, singing one of my favourite church songs, and take my seat to the side where three men are seated – one of them is Bishop Silawuli, a tall, good-humoured man who is always happy to remind everyone that he is over 60.

The bishop's newly ordained wife, Pastor Silawuli, and their daughter, Nkuli, take up two seats in the front row, closest to the pulpit. The pulpit is on a slightly raised platform, closely resembling a podium. Nkuli leads almost all the singing in the church – her velvet and crushed ice voice is one of the reasons her ministry is that of worship; the other reasons being her love for the church and God. And when Nkuli is singing, backed up in melody by the small group of women and men at Upper Hall, all else can be easily forgotten. But they have a lone microphone, so even though they have strong and beautiful singing voices, they cannot be heard talking on the podium as the *kwaito* continues to blast unapologetically just outside. It is through this mic that the day's word of encouragement is delivered by *Umvangeli* (Evangelist) Ngqula. Testimonies are given by the congregants, following this small sermon, until 11 a.m.

Services at God's Love Ministries begin at 11 a.m., so I leave home on a Taxify again at 10:40 a.m. This time we are driving towards the far end of the township, where Alexandra meets Marlboro. Most of this side is the old Alexandra, where up to three face-brick, farm-style houses would stand in a yard. The owners of these homes started to rent out rooms built within the yards to tenants (Bonner & Nieftagodien 2008: 83) and came to be known as *bo Ma-stand* (stand holders). Now, most of these former 'stands' are filled with different types of structures – between small rooms and shacks. So many are there that one cannot, without walking through the full distance of the stands, see the houses of old. I do, however, notice that there are still one or two stands that have been kept in their original state save for walls built around them.

I get off at the end of a driveway where five cars are parked nose-to-nose. There is hardly any pavement, since some residents have raised buildings for their small businesses on the little space they could find. A bright blue crèche takes up the pavement where I get off, and I make my way up the driveway to the old Alexandra house that has now also been turned into a crèche. God's Love has a keyboard, microphones and speakers, so following their sound into the newly renovated crèche is not difficult. The homes around the crèche play their music quietly, or so it seems because of the booming voices coming from the crèche. An usher I recognise as Pastor Patrick Sixoka's brother stands at the door to greet and direct me to my chair. This old house has been divided into two rooms, the first of which is used by God's Love as their Sunday reception area.

It takes some adjusting to the stuffy smell, as I look around to see if they have opened any windows. It is a small space, fitting for the number of congregants, who give me beaming smiles as I make my way to a seat in the front. Pastor Fuzeka is a ball of energy, participating in every part of the church programme.

She is the chorus leader, co-pastor, intercessor, evangelist and councillor at the church. She is standing in the front singing when I take my seat. She wears a blue shirt tucked into a black pencil skirt and has her hair in a relaxed, low ponytail. I have never seen her without a smile. So welcoming is this smile, through which a strong alto lead comes, that most congregants come to the front of the church to dance. She stops singing occasionally to let the keyboard take over as she joins in the dancing. After she signals a 'time-out' with her hands, people start to take their seats and the keyboard plays a little softer. 'Amen, *bazalwane* [born again/saved of the Lord]!' she shouts through the mic.[13] The congregation greets her with a resounding 'Amen'. It is 11:30 a.m.

To get to Red Sea Ministries is quick and easy, as I get a lift from Mathero – one of the women who attends church there. She picks me up at 9:30 a.m. for a 10:00 a.m. service. We drive down busy Roosevelt Street and turn into 16th Avenue, where Mathero slows down to manoeuvre amongst the street humps and people walking in the road because of the lack of a pavement. When we finally reach 16th Avenue and Selbourne, we are further delayed by taxis stopping to let people either on or off, but it is no matter because we are only one street away. At 17th Avenue, we turn left and begin to scan the pavements on either side for a parking space. Mathero takes one on a driveway to our right, after a shirtless young man beckons us to the space and assures us that church people are always welcome. We park and thank him, and of course promise to pray for him too. The building we are walking to is Phutha Dichaba, a community centre built by the famously loved native of Alexandra, Linda Twala. It stands quite majestically, at two face-brick storeys, over the small houses, shacks, and *zozo* huts that occupy the street.[14] The building has two uniformed security guards standing at its red and gold gates. We greet and walk past them, and then past the largest hall in the building where one of Alexandra's Methodist Church satellite branches holds its Sunday meetings. I pause to peek at the red, black and white uniforms bouncing to the beat of a melodious song, and fail to resist the temptation to sing along. The Methodist Church was my grandmother's home, and my first memory of church. Then we walk up the stairs and down a long passage to the boardroom, where Red Sea Ministries have their church meetings. The congregants are in prayer when we walk in. Some are kneeling at their chairs, while others walk about the room shouting 'in Jesus' name!' I take a seat on the far right, grateful for the cool air coming through the open window. A song begins and the MC comes to the front to greet and welcome everyone. We are encouraged to shake hands with each other as another song – 'Wenze Kahle Wafika Nawe'('It Was Good of You to Come') – is sung.[15] The MC, Sifiso, then asks for praise songs, which are accompanied by handclapping and dancing. It is after three songs, at 10:45 a.m., that the MC now happily announces, 'church is in session, bazalwane'.

When church is in session

There are a few things that the four churches I am introducing have in common besides their being Pentecostal Charismatic churches. The first is that they all have relatively small groups of congregants: Living Waters with the most at around 30 adults and God's Love with the fewest at 9 adults. Secondly, none of them have built structures in which they congregate. They are all, thirdly, mostly populated by women – this is the case at both the churches led by men and those led by women. And lastly, all four churches have similar singing, worship and sermon styles.

Singing, or praising, is led by one or two 'worship leaders' – that is, those who have been blessed with very good and strong voices, so good that they are able to get other congregants into the spirit. Praise time is filled with energy as people clap, sing loudly, smile and dance. Some go to the front of the church to show off dance moves as the rest of the church cheers them on. Children who go forward to dance are given the loudest cheers. Worship is essential to all services, as the pastors always stress the importance of prayer and getting aligned with the will of God. Worship is also a time to thank – not ask from – God for all that the worshipper has. A slow, spiritually infused song is sung by the congregants to get them into a prayerful state. It is when the song slows down even more that congregants will begin to pray, hands lifted, eyes closed, crying, then kneeling and chanting.

It is hard to tell what each person prays for or about, because they all speak at once. Everyone prays in the language that they are most comfortable with. There are, for instance, times when you may hear Tsonga or Venda from some, where the most generally used language is English or Xhosa. Many members of Pentecostal Charismatic churches pray in tongues – a language believed to be a holy connection between the worshipper and God, especially holy because it is prompted by the Holy Spirit and only God will understand what is being said. And sermons are delivered by the pastor of the church as the last event of the Sunday programme. Sermons last an average of one hour. The congregants are seated while the pastor speaks, and sermons are mostly introduced and concluded by a prayer from the pastor or one of the congregants.

Living Waters Ministries

Before Pastor Nyathi takes his stand at the wooden pulpit in the front, it is his wife, Pastor Rose Nyathi, who addresses the church. She begins a song, which all join in singing. As Rose does this, she picks up a white shawl with frills on both ends and blue Hebrew lettering embroidered on its front. She uses this shawl to cover her head and shoulders. The other women in the church then begin to cover themselves as well. Shawls which had been on their laps during the service now cover their heads or shoulders or both, as they stand to watch Rose walk slowly up to the pulpit. Rose opens the Bible to read a verse that she explains in a style of teaching to the congregants, who keep nodding with approval and responding with an 'Amen'. When she does not get an Amen, she prompts one by saying, 'Amen, *bazalwane*' or '*niyangizwa* [do you hear/understand me], *bazalwane*?'

At the end of her sermon, Rose gives a chance to anyone in the congregation to come up and give a prophetic word. 'I feel that we have some prophecies and don't want to leave anyone out before *Umfundisi* [the pastor] comes up, share what God has placed in your hearts', are the words she uses to encourage prophecies. It works, as three women stand up to share what God has told them about the church, life in general, and specific people within the congregation.

Upper Hall Ministries

A specific call for prophecies is not made when I am at this church. Instead, the word of encouragement shared by *Umvangeli* Ngquka is taken up as one by the three women who stand to give their testimonies. They each thank God for the words that were placed in Nqguka's heart. They affirm every word he said by giving examples of how their own lives, and the very events of the week, are confirmations that God sees them and wants to heal them, or make them whole, or help their families get saved. One of the women asks for prayers, as a child in their family has gone missing after going to a party with her friends.

The women at Upper Hall are somewhat conservatively dressed. Most are in long skirts and sleeves. Those who wear knee-length skirts cover their legs with shawls when they sit. None have their heads covered. The dress code at Upper Hall is formal skirts instead of jeans, and heels or fancy pumps in place of beach sandals and *takkies* (sneakers).

Nkuli, in a long floral maxi-dress, stands with a song to make announcements. Upper Hall is organising a Christmas event where they will have 'secret Santa'. Each member is asked to buy a thoughtful gift that costs no more than R150. Members are also encouraged to keep saving money for a special trip to be taken to the main church in the Eastern Cape in a few months to come. Then Nkuli asks all to stand and welcome Bishop Silawuli to the front, as he gets ready to deliver his sermon.

God's Love Ministries

At God's Love the only formally dressed women are Pastor Fuzeka and Mrs Sexoka (Pastor Patrick's wife). The rest are in jeans, *takkies* and varying styles of skirts and dresses. Pastor Bongani, Pastor Patrick's brother, has now taken over as MC and song leader, giving Pastor Fuzeka a chance to prepare herself for the sermon she is to deliver. Most of the church members are family, and many of them have attended or are attending divinity and pastoral classes so that they can be ordained, too. Pastor Fuzeka was ordained on spiritual merit – her calling was considered obvious by the pastor who led the church before her. Her qualifications are in finance, and she is busy with her honours degree at the University of South Africa (Unisa).

Before calling Fuzeka to deliver her sermon, Bongani calls Patrick up to give a special word. 'Special' because Patrick likes to thank each person present for their contribution to the church and the service: none more than his wife, to whom he is forever grateful for her support, love and taking care of their children. On this day, I am one of the people to whom Patrick feels grateful and by whom his church has been blessed. 'Special' also because Patrick's greatest passion is 'soul-winning', and he uses this time to remind the members of the church that this should be their goal, too.[16] After a worship song, for which every person in the room stands, Fuzeka comes to the portable pulpit (assembled quickly by another one of Patrick's brothers) to give her sermon for the day.

Red Sea Ministries

As in the case of God's Love, most people at Red Sea Ministries are related. Unlike the practice at God's Love, the pastor here dresses in smart casual clothing, and sometimes even wears *takkies* with her dresses. The women follow their pastor's fashion sense quite closely – in stylish jeans, boob-tube dresses and above-the-knee skirts. At this church, all are expected to be smart, but there are no rules about revealing too much, so one is likely to see more skin than at the other three churches.

All the women who stand to give their testimonies read and explain Bible verses, what these verses mean to them, and how they apply to their lives. In fact, every part of the programme at this service is accompanied by a Bible verse: a psalm for praise, Malachi for offering, Revelations 12 to encourage testimonies.[17] Mathero gives testimony about the sense of community and love she has found in the church. She feels that there is more support amongst the women at Red Sea Ministries than she receives at home.

This is the kind of testimony I am to hear often when visiting these churches. Some of the women were not born in Johannesburg and go to rural areas in other provinces during holidays. To them, the churches they attend are their place of nourishing family values. Others, even while having family in Johannesburg, feel somewhat alienated from those families and prefer to build relationships with the other members of the church.

The sermons

So far, I have provided a joyful entry into each of these churches. Church is a happy place, but following in Sara Ahmed's footsteps of being a 'killjoy' (2017), I must provide a critique of happiness and happy places to question the authority that uses happiness to impose its will and as a justification of oppression (Ahmed 2010). In this section, I will give an overview of how the pastors address women and define their gender identities. In discussing all the sermons, I will be addressing how the different pastors employ discursive strategies to reproduce, challenge or inflect gender ideologies. The most common discursive strategies include justification and legitimation of the social order, and a denial and concealment of inequality (Van Dijk 1993). I also wish to elaborate on two specific events. The first is the reciting of a poem that was written by Pastor Mabaso, who is a lay minister at Upper Hall Ministries, and read on the Sunday after Women's Day (a South African public holiday) in 2019. The second is a special ceremony that Bishop Silawuli performed at Red Sea Ministries that was followed by Pastor Xoli's sermon. On this day, in September 2019, a wedding announcement was made and all who were a part of the bride-to-be's life were invited to attend.

Pastor Mabaso's poem

This is a section of the poem read by Pastor Mabaso at Upper Hall Ministries, which she dedicated to women:

> Beautiful like the Rose of Sharon.
> Beauty and splendour and sweet and gracious,
> You are the true subjects of heaven
> Pure like rainwater
> Humble like a dove – majestic like a morning star!
> Warm like a blanket
> Tasty like a Kit-Kat chocolate
> *Waze wamuhle ntombi!* [You're so beautiful!]
> Holy of holies,

Rooted and grounded and lovely woman of God.
The woman of Psalm 31
Woman of courage,
Of wisdom, of kindness
Woman of impact
God-fearing woman,
Mother-nation
Mother of the sons and daughters of the Kingdom
The crying shoulder, the heart of worship, the
pioneer of pioneers.
Voice of the voiceless, the divinity, the eye of the
blind

> Woman of God…

This poem especially stood out for me because of the way it describes and celebrates women. I say 'celebrate' based on the reaction of the women who attended the service where it was recited. The poem gives a normative embodiment of women as beauty, spirituality, motherhood and strength of character. The woman described in this poem can have it all, yet chooses humility and service. Her place is with God and with the sons and daughters that she mothers in the way of God. Her beauty is in her purity and heavenliness. She stands against injustice, for those who cannot stand for themselves. She is also ready to hear the cries of others, and is creative and a leader of worship. This poem is an illustration of the terms Sylvia Tamale (2014) uses to describe sexuality, and encompasses the question of respectability too (see also Horn 2006; Hungwe 2006; Mupotsa 2014, 2015a, 2015b; Tamale 2016). The woman celebrated here is part of a construct of expectations – conservative, respectable and loved. It is these very expectations that are raised within most of the sermons I have listened to.

When women and descriptions of women are clothed and covered in prescriptive ideas of beauty, it becomes a discursive colonisation of their femininity. This poem, written and recited to celebrate women, ends up being a means to imprison them further. It is women who must live up to this exaggerated celebration of beauty and of strength that feels no pain. Such constructions use gendered differences to create what Ahmed

(2010) calls 'conditional happiness'. This is happiness for the subdued woman whose happiness is dependent upon meeting the conditions that define the happiness of others. The woman's duty is to ensure that those before her are pleased and are happy before she can finally declare herself happy too. The woman herself in this poem is conditional, celebrated for her success at building and pleasing men, children and God. The wedding announcement extends this conditioning and more explicitly sets out the hierarchies of happiness and the conditions to be fulfilled.

The sound of wedding bells

Mathapelo is officially engaged, save for a blessing of this engagement by the men and women of God. That is the reason the small Red Sea Ministries' boardroom space is filled to capacity. There is excitement in the air, as the room tinkles with beautifully dressed women and men. Before the service began, much was prepared, including intricate decorations for the boardroom, which is normally left in its usual state except for moving the table to the front and arranging the chairs in rows. On this special day, more chairs have been requested from the management of Phutha Dichaba, the community centre where this service is being held. They are still arranged in rows, leaving space for an aisle, but very little space is left between the rows so that more black plastic chairs can fit in this time. The table in the front is not only covered in a tablecloth, but an arrangement of colourful roses is centred on it in a vase. There is also white draping around the room, and the chairs have been covered in the same crisp white.

As more people – neighbours, friends, extended family, colleagues and supporters from other churches – arrive, Mathapelo sits shyly at the back of the room next to her new fiancé. She is wearing a black, knee-length A-line dress, black heels, and has her head covered in a colourful *doek* (headscarf). I jokingly ask her if this is going to be her new *makoti* look. She says that she just feels like being different on this day. I am thinking of the 'Makoti Chic' signposted by Danai Mupotsa in 'Becoming Girl-Woman-Bride' (2015a: 81), as the bride's 'self-styling enables a scene or event in which the bride is not possessed by anyone, unless by herself, since the bride is her own ideal and love object'. Mathapelo's fiancé, Calem, sits quietly beside her waiting for our small girl-talk to be translated for him as he is not well-versed in South African languages.

As every person present sings along to an array of praise songs, with Sifiso (the usual MC) running the programme, even more people arrive to celebrate Mathapelo: so many more that having the table with flowers in front no longer makes sense. The table is moved out to make room for three more rows of chairs and is replaced by the portable pulpit from God's Love. More chairs are also placed at the side of the room, and Mathapelo's closest family is moved to them. And as even more people come for the celebration, chairs are placed just outside – this is where the children now sit, with Sibongile, who runs the Sunday school at God's Love. When every person is seated and testimonies have been heard, the service begins.

Bishop Silawuli asks the couple to come to the front, where two chairs have now been placed for them. Sifiso takes on the role of translator now, as Silawuli speaks Xhosa. Silawuli asks a family member, preferably an uncle, to sit between the couple. It is Mathapelo's aunt who obliges this request. The uncle instead stands facing the bishop. He confirms all that is being asked: the lobola has been agreed upon by both families and yes, has been paid; the family acknowledges and accepts this union; they welcome Calem with open arms. When these questions have been answered to Silawuli's satisfaction, he then allows for the couple to sit together, with no one in between them. We are ready for a union!

Maria Frahm-Arp (2010) describes the practices at the Grace Bible Church megachurch in Soweto as an example of how African traditions are merged with Christianity, so that members are encouraged not to completely 'break from the past'. At Grace Bible Church, lobola is not only supported but encouraged, and symbolises a man's ability and willingness to take care of his wife and to fully commit to the union. In the case of the churches I am discussing, lobola is also encouraged and the extended family is recognised as an important part of this process. In some African traditions, the uncles of the bride and groom play a pivotal role during the lobola negotiations, and are also called on as mediators should there be some trouble within the marriage. This confirms what Frahm-Arp describes as the marrying of some African cultures with Christianity by Pentecostal churches in townships. Bishop Silawuli relies on Mathapelo's uncle to legitimise this union by asking for his testimony before this special ceremony can go on.

Silawuli's sermon mainly addresses Calem and his responsibilities. Mathapelo is spoken for by her uncle at first, and then by her fiancé. Silawuli asks Calem to stand up and speak. Calem thanks everyone for coming to support them on this day, and assures us that he plans to love and take good care of his wife-to-be. All applaud this declaration. Mathapelo is not asked to stand or say anything.

Mathapelo's expected silence is furthered when Silawuli says, 'once the family agrees and accepts you, then it's a done deal!' He communicates an agreement of marriage as one that is between the groom and the bride's family. By saying this, Mathapelo – her voice, her agency and her decisions – is annulled. The pastor's speech places Mathapelo as the passive receiver of the advances made by Calem and accepted by her family. He goes on to say: 'this man prayed to God and the angels went with him. *Kungumusa kaNkulunkulu ukuthi isoka lifike endlini. Kuyajajulwa kwelo khaya.* [It is by the mercy of God that a single man arrives at a woman's home. It brings great joy to that family]'.

Silawuli then asks all pastors present to come forward and bless the engagement ring. They all stand around the couple and pray over them and their new union. It is then that Calem can place the ring on Mathapelo's finger. The wedding date is set for May 2020, but the couple is now free to live together. Frahm-Arp (2010) accounts for this blessing of lobola and engagements as a response to couples who want to be together but cannot necessarily afford a big wedding yet. They are given freedom from celibacy when lobola is recognised in the church as a 'blessed union'. In fact, Silawuli stresses many times that this union will not be recognised if lobola has not been paid, hence his calling of Mathapelo's uncle to confirm it.

The blessing of the rings is another happy occasion, obviously made so by the ululating in the boardroom. Yet it is also an occasion that calls upon our questioning of power. Mathapelo is physically present in the boardroom, but absent in voice. It is up to Silawuli and her uncle to legitimise this union. To use Mupotsa's words, Mathapelo 'should have the opportunity to speak on…her own behalf' but her agency is compromised twice – by the lobola negotiations and by the church's blessings that follow.[18] All in the name of happiness.

But Pentecostal Charismatic churches are not a site of homogeneous beliefs and ideologies. There are complexities, different voices and internal tensions or even conflicts within their practices and beliefs. These were evidenced by a sermon delivered by Pastor Xoli after Bishop Silawuli's blessing of the rings.

Same bells, different ideologies

The sermon delivered by Pastor Xoli contradicts almost everything said and done by Silawuli in the blessing of the rings. What she delivers not only gives Mathapelo her voice back, but questions the role played by men in marriage. She speaks of a need for men to heal. Men need healing from their need to dominate women, which Xoli says is against Biblical principles. This is followed by silence from the congregation. But this silence does not deter Pastor Xoli, who goes on to read the story of human creation in Genesis, from which she signposts:

> Lithi Izwi [the Word says], man is to have dominance over the earth and all its creatures. Akekho umuntu [there is no one person] who has been given authority to dominate over another human being. So, lento le yamadoda [this thing of men] thinking they have authority over abafazi [women] is evil and against the Word of God.

Now receiving applause and amens from the congregation, Pastor Xoli carries on speaking about healing and partnership. She talks about the upbringing of men by men, women and communities that teaches them about strength, especially physical strength, instead of teaching them about the 'heart which controls the issues of life'.[19] She gives examples of men, from her own experiences and from the Bible, who failed to connect with their emotions and receive the healing they need, instead turning to their physical strength for the answers. Xoli describes the heart that has not been healed from the past, which hurts and pains, as a cancer that eats up society. To Calem she gives advice to find his healing in God, and to receive counselling as he begins his new life as a husband. And to the congregation she explains that her sermon is directed at men because, unlike women, they do not cry but instead harbour wounds in their souls, wounds that bleed by hurting the women and children in their lives:

> For in a world of madness where men don't cry…
> those men cry by killing their children. Do you
> see that men do bleed? They bleed by killing and
> raping women. It is about time men cry! Stop
> expecting women to carry you – bleed and cry.
> Find your corner with God and heal.

Xoli begins her sermon by dispelling the 'myth' of male dominance, giving Mathapelo her equal place by Calem's side. In the rest of the sermon, she addresses issues that are plaguing South Africa – especially the highly publicised cases of femicide, gender-based violence and child abuse. It is interesting that she chooses to highlight these issues at a wedding engagement celebration. It could be because she knows that the audience will be bigger than her usual congregation of about 10 women. Or it could be due to her feeling that this is the best time to talk about pain, because many cases of gender-based violence are caused by intimate partners; hence her advising the future groom to seek counselling to avoid hurting his bride. Whatever Xoli's reasoning, she delivers a sermon that denounces toxic masculinity and the processes of socialisation that build it. This pastor also implores her audience to recognise the importance of emotion, as opposed to seeing it as secondary to logic and physical strength (see Dillard 2000). But, more importantly, in a process of transitivity, Pastor Xoli assigns men the responsibility for their own feelings and actions, just as Audre Lorde asserts that 'Black men are not so passive that they must have Black women speak for them' (Lorde 2007: 46), act for them or make excuses for masculine behaviour that endangers Black women.

Women in the pulpit

Pastor Xoli and Pastor Fuzeka use their respective pulpits to empower women – in some or even most cases. They employ discursive strategies to oppose masculinism and promote feminism. They also resist the notion of a 'natural' gender order, stating that God is not for tradition. In a call to feminise the church, Pastor Xoli foregrounds emotions in women as their greatest standing with God: 'teach your daughters to wail. God wants to see your tears, but the bottle is empty. The church needs healing, the church needs women who are not afraid to cry to God.'

Pastor Fuzeka's focus in most of her sermons is on the building of family – and upholding the African tradition of keeping up relationships with extended family members: '*singabantu abamnyama* [we are Black], we can't create our own corners. *Sinobuntu* [we have ubuntu] and we help each other. We can't create our own families and close out our extended family.'

Fuzeka also uses feminised metaphors to describe the nature of God to her congregants. This goes against the general Christian grain of believing that God is a (white) man, depicted in imagery that creates the hierarchical structures through which men and women see the world (Daly 1985; Johnson 1984; Shooter 2014; Whitehead 2012). In the story of salvation that Fuzeka tells her congregation, she gives a picture of God as female and the church as her prized possession:

> *Kukho umama oye wawisa i-ring yakhe phakathi kwomjelo wamanzi amdaka. Uthe lomama maka cinga ukujika, wabuya wacinga la-ring enhle kuye, futhi ethandekayo. Wabe engena lomama kulomjelo…wayikhupha i-ring. Walibala tu ngokunuka, nokugula ngoba afuna into ayithandayo…Wuye ke UThixo kuthi bazalwane. Ufana nalomama okhuphe i-ring from the sewer. Uyasikhipha ekuncoleni, namanyala wezono zethu. UThixo Uyasithanda bazalwane.*
>
> [There was once a woman who dropped her ring in a sewer. Every time this woman thought about turning away, she would remember her beautiful ring, and how valuable it was to her. So, she got

into the sewer and brought out the ring. She forgot completely about the smell, the dirt, the germs, because she wanted what she found so beautiful and valuable. That is God to us. God is like the woman who took her ring from the sewer. God takes us out of the dirt and filth of our sins. God loves us.]

Both women pastors express a disdain for 'blessers' (rich men who have transactional relationships with younger women) in their sermons, but also warn the women in their congregations against falling for the charms of blessers. In one of her sermons, Pastor Fuzeka provides her own arrival in Johannesburg as an example of not allowing money and success to lure her into 'temptation'. She explains that she opted to move out of her 'uncle's' (a family friend's) home and into a badly constructed shack when he started making sexual advances to her:

Ndamjonga ngamehlo ndamxelela ukuba ngeke ubone lamanyala kimi. Ndakhetha ukuhlala emkhukhwini ndingenakudla. Jonga into andenzela yona uThixo. Ngiyasebenza, ngi right ngoba ngihale uSatane. Nawe ungenza njalo, ubone izibusiso zikaNkunlunkulu.

[I looked him straight in the eye and said, 'I will never do something so obscene and immoral.' I opted to stay in a shack, with no food. Now look how God has rewarded me. I have a good job now because I resisted the devil. You can do the same, you will reap the blessings of God.]

And Pastor Xoli tells a similar narrative of blessings that come from resisting the devil, when she gives accounts of the women she saw 'sitting on the boss's lap' to get promotions or special favours during her time in the corporate world.

The women pastors have a strong leaning towards a liberation hermeneutics, using their own and their congregants' experiences to build an image of God as a liberator of women. They even feminise texts of the Bible, and God too, to provide a sense of empowerment for the women they preach to, making sure that they do not feel responsible for bad male behaviour. However, even as I see the intention to empower women with narratives of escaping sexual harassment, rape and sexual coercion, it is problematic for such simplistic views of women and their plight to be the only examples used in women's pulpits.

I am reminded of an episode of *Scandal*, a Shonda Rhimes television series that in South Africa is called *The Fixer*, which depicts a similar narrative.[20] The only woman in this story who, as the two pastors suggest, 'resists the corporate male devil' by refusing to have sex with her boss, ends her life after the same man blacklists her with every firm at which she might try to get a job. The women who fail to resist the devil live – granted, in a state of guilt for how their friend ended her life, but they live nonetheless to build the careers they have dreamt of. This episode shows that it does nothing for women to be set against each other as rivals, 'failures' and 'victors'. No woman wins in these scenarios: they were never made for women to win. So, I am relieved that the two pastors came out of their ordeals unscathed and blessed, but their narratives conceal the power relations that position women as targets of toxic masculine power.

Patricia Hill Collins talks of the four domains of power, namely the 'structural domain', which organises oppression; the 'disciplinary domain', which manages it; the 'hegemonic domain', which serves to justify oppression; and the 'interpersonal domain', the main influence on everyday lived experience that results in individual perceptions (2000: 18). Rather than questioning the structural and disciplinary modes of power, the two women pastors unwittingly enter the hegemonic domain of justifying the oppression of women. And in the interpersonal domain, they reinforce the 'cult of femininity' that has women caught in discourses of empowerment that are in fact not empowering at all, since they ensure that women adapt to the existing structural systems rather than transform them (Gqola 2007: 115–116). It is the very structures of patriarchy that authorise men to abuse women's bodies which should be questioned, rather than the choices made by women in these situations to survive in their male worlds.

Men in the pulpit

Pastor Nyathi has his sermon on a laptop, which stands on the pulpit. His overall nature is quite animated, but he stands still to read the words on the laptop, pausing only to add thoughts to his prepared speech. Bishop Silawuli has a page of notes on his pulpit but does not stay in one place when preaching; he walks around the front of the room – sometimes jumping or kneeling to stress certain points.

Employing narrative, argument and transitivity, both these men take the side of tradition in their constructions of femininity. Bishop Silawuli, talking about marriage, specifically states: '50/50 is not the Christian way. It is against the Bible.' The term 50/50 goes back to popular culture at the start of this century, when pop music was promoting the idea of gender equality. In South Africa, there was a specific answer to the equality of the sexes by the famously loved *kwaito* stars Mandoza and Mdu, who released '50/50' (2001) in response to the American pop group Destiny Child's 'Independent Woman'.[21] The lyrics of '50/50' suggest that women should begin to contribute to household expenses and cover half of the bill since they consider themselves 'independent'. From 2001 onwards, all things relating to gender equality have become popularly umbrellaed under the term 50/50. Men use the term to suggest that women should pay for more things, and women use the term to ask for equal treatment in all spheres relating to the genders.

It is unclear which definition of 50/50 Bishop Silawuli uses in his sermon. I would argue, however, that in any form his statement is traditionalist. By polarising where women should stand, he suggests that they should be on the traditional 'receiving end': receiving of male dominance and of monetary treatment. To define what is Christian or unChristian for women gives them two choices: be on the side of God and accept a lower status, or oppose that side to achieve equal standing with men.

Both pastors present the idea of a 'Christian' as one who does not challenge patriarchal norms, and the 'non-Christian' as one who challenges injustices against women. Their sermons also conceal patriarchal ideologies, using a softer version of patriarchy that gives women responsibilities and roles that are traditional in nature. In this way, they construct an identity for women that does not threaten the existing male power and dominance (Nadar 2009b). A spiritual woman, according to their sermons, is one who allows men their traditional roles and accepts that what they say is God's doing regarding women's plight. These sermons provide an example of how the Bible and spirituality are used to further subjugate a group, and contradict the idea of a Jesus who liberates and restores women's dignity (see Baloyi 2008a, 2008b, 2010; Oraegbunam 2006).

Pastor Nyathi addresses two young women in the church as follows:

> I am taking you two with me when we drive out to the outing. See they are twins, and I wish for one of them to marry my son so that I may have a greater chance of being a grandfather to twins. I wish for boys, though. Boys will ensure that the Nyathi name can live on.

Nyathi claims the two women in a seemingly joking manner. He takes an identity that belongs to them as one that can be exploited for his own aims. They are twins, and so one of them should be able to bear twins for his son. His statement not only presumes their heterosexuality, but also the two women's willingness and desire to be a part of his heteronormative family. And he presumes that, as women, they will one day bear children, just as Pastor Mabaso's poem quoted earlier in this chapter does. One of them will marry his son and bear him twins. An honour seems to be bestowed upon them: an honour clothed in the respectability of marriage and childbearing for and by their spiritual leader. The twins laugh shyly, casting their eyes down and nodding in agreement with what their pastor has proposed.

It is not only twin children who are expected from this fantastic union, but boys, who will carry the Nyathi name and keep it alive. This statement annuls the importance of the twins for Pastor Nyathi. It is what they can bring that takes precedence. And it is obvious that the children they can bear are what is even more important. Boys will carry the Nyathi name. Boys will preserve the life of the name. Women are only good for carrying and delivering the boys who will carry the name.

The second time I visited Upper Hall, Bishop Silawuli asked all the women in the church – which is mostly made up of women – to take seats in the front. He insisted that they do this as acknowledgement of their importance to the growth of the church. *Omama* (women who are married, relatively older or with children) were especially encouraged by the bishop to take up leadership positions, considering their role as 'leaders and managers of the house', showing again a construction of femininity in normative and hegemonic patriarchal terms. The separation of the types of women here gives us an idea of respectability and how it plays itself out at Upper Hall. As Jessica Horn (2006) points out, this is the idea of a leader and manager who stands for domesticity, as these women are named leaders of the house – not in general society. Their heterosexuality, ability to bear children and age are what legitimates their standing as leaders.

Here Bishop Silawuli does not polarise femininity according to Christianity. He makes the necessary assumption that all who are present are already Christian and in line with the will of God he spoke of the week before. It is the choices that they have made which now stand out and give them the right to claim leadership. These choices are those of childbearing and marriage. Having children and being part of a heterosexual family unit brings about the necessary respect (see Horn 2006; Tamale 2014) and honour (see Hungwe 2006). Silawuli does not necessarily denounce the women who do not have children or are not married, but he is epideictic in his argument for the admiration of women who have conformed to traditional standards. He makes a public call for them to be given praise and admired by his church.

Pastor Nyathi, however, expresses his dissatisfaction with what he calls the 'tradition' of only ordaining women who are married:

> For once I would like to ordain a single woman. We are always ordaining a husband and wife for church leadership. Women do not have to be married to be leaders in the church. Show us your commitment at the home cell so that we can name you a leader too – with or without a husband.

From the mouths of babes – *Bomthandazo*

I have described the different types of women who attend the Alexandra churches I visited at the beginning of this chapter, though not in individual detail. You should by now have an idea of how they dress and present themselves. At God's Love Ministries, the women are conservatively dressed and express more humility than at the other three churches. This could be due to their being working class – most of them are labourers, cleaners and nannies. Their woman co-pastor, Pastor Fuzeka, came to Johannesburg from the Eastern Cape to do a cleaning job at a bank. Hers is a story that attracts the women of her church to the prospect of a fairy-tale-like upward mobility. Fuzeka had worked as a cleaner for one year when her friendly nature and hard work got the attention of management, who promoted her to tea-making in the management offices. During the months that these managers of the bank got to know her, they liked her so much that she was given an opportunity to further her studies at the bank's expense. It was when she was halfway through her bachelor of commerce (BCom) degree at Unisa that she began her training as a bank teller – which is now her permanent employment. She now has a degree and is working towards her BCom Honours.

At Upper Hall Ministries there is a mixture of education levels and socioeconomic classes. Thando has an electrical engineering degree and has begun her courses for a master's degree. She works for a parastatal and has recently been promoted. Maria works at the same parastatal as a tea-maker, and is currently doing her matric through an adult basic education and training programme. Both women are 32 years old. The women at Living Waters Ministries have a similar social constitution to those at Upper Hall. Their jobs range from corporate administration to university students and cleaners. And the Red Sea Ministries women all have a form of or are working towards higher education qualifications. Three of the women have a master's degree and one is reading towards her PhD. All of them have professional careers in various disciplines.

This section of the chapter focuses on these women. I will be discussing how they relate to the sermons they receive and the practices of their church. Issues that are important to them will be the main discussion points and will highlight for us how they perceive themselves in the church and society, and how they define their gender identities.

Desire: Marriage, heterosexual love

>]I want love, Tumi, I want to get a call from reception to collect flowers from my husband. *Kebatla hoba happy. Kebatla motho who will love my kids as much as I do. A man ozongithatha nemithwalo yami!* [I want to be happy. I want someone who will love my kids as much as I do. A man who will take me with my baggage!]
>
> — Lerato, 28-year-old procurement buyer

I begin this section with a quote from Lerato because it brings to our attention a few things about the Pentecostal women from Alexandra whom I present in this book. The first is the obvious subject of this section – a desire for marriage. The second is the heteronormative way in which the women construct love relationships and see themselves within these constructions. A heterosexual union within the institution of marriage is their fanciful means of achieving a happy ending. In relaying to me what happiness means to her, Lerato prompted in me a need to ask the other women in the Upper Hall group what turned out to be an awkward question, followed by uncomfortable and quizzical silences. All the women in this group are single, apart from Sibongile, whose husband attends the same church.

I asked the single women if, like Lerato, marriage is something they want. This question was followed by a long and perplexed silence. The women shifted in their chairs, stealing questioning glances at me and then at each other. It was Magauta, 47 years old and divorced, who finally broke the initial silence by turning the question on me:

> Ha ke nahane hore ho na le mosadi oka reng yena ha batle lenyalo. Mo hona re kabe re eputsa maka. Ngqono wena o explain why oka botsa question e so…unless you're…Heh…Tumi ha o batle ho nyaloa?

> [I don't think there is any woman who does not want to be married. We would be lying to ourselves by saying that. Maybe you should explain why you're asking this question to begin with...unless you're... wait...Tumi, you don't want to be married?]

I answered the question honestly, explaining, after some prompting, the reasons I do not believe that the institution of marriage is one I could commit myself to. After an even longer silence, Sibongile, the married woman in the group, spoke up, offering a more 'acceptable' explanation to the group of puzzled women:

> Listen everybody, I know what's happening here and we all just need to calm down. Tumi is just tired and has too much on her plate especially with all this studying. *Futhi sibakhona leso s'khathi la umuntu azitshela ukuthi hayi ngi-right ngomshado, but into engiyaziyo ukuthi siyadlula* [there is a time when everybody feels as if they don't want marriage, but what I know is that this time passes], so for now it's fine to feel that way. Once she's done and her degree is submitted, she will find a good man who will change her mind. *Kwazibani?* [who knows?] Maybe next year *sizozwa sekuth'wa nazo* [we will be hearing] wedding bells!

To which everybody applauded and started singing wedding songs. What a relief to know that there is hope for my happiness after all!

It is the taken-for-grantedness of the desire for marriage by researchers (Frahm-Arp 2012; Mhongo 2013; Posel, Rudwick & Casale 2011; Rudwick & Posel 2013) who try to answer the question of what stands in the way of Black women marrying, and by the women I speak to, that is of interest here. The reaction of the women at Upper Hall, and Magauta's response, show the homogeneous understanding of women and desire. Every woman wants a happily-ever-after with a man. No consideration is given to lesbian women who may or may not want to marry, gender non-conforming persons, or heterosexual women like myself who do not embrace that desire.

When I state my position on the matter of marriage, and give reasons why I do not want it, letting them know that I have given the matter much thought, my statement causes them discomfort. Ahmed (2010) speaks of the idea of heterosexual marriage unions as a naturalised desire. Women are taught that to be good, to want good, involves marrying and building a family. My statement of wanting the contrary was seen by the women in the Upper Hall group as a deviation, and 'deviations from nature become deviations from the common good' (Ahmed 2010: 58). The group's reaction to the deviant in this case is to silence what does not come across as natural. Taken-for-granted desire stems from and is a naturalised heterenormativity. To see heterosexuality and to justify and promote the natural heterosexual woman, and to define what is natural for such a woman, does the inverse of what 'drag, butch, femme, transgender, transsexual persons' do, in Judith Butler's terms. Where queer persons bring into question what we consider normal and real, and so present possibilities of embodiment that show us that the normal and real 'are not written in stone' (Butler 2004: 29), heteronormativity anxiously means to silence any question of possibility outside of what it defines as a normal and real femininity. Indeed, between the queer embodiment and the 'normal' hetererosexual lies a possibility, many possibilities, of being (a woman): possibilities that should and do include choices of being outside of what is considered natural. However, such possibilities are not seen as possiblities by the heteronormative eye, but as an uncomfortable and perplexing willing away of happiness.

So, Sibongile goes about bringing me back onto the path of happiness (see Ahmed 2010, 2014b). She explains to the women that I speak out of fatigue – for my natural want and need for 'good' could not possibly speak this way. On the path laid out for me is a good man who will change my mind. Change my will.

It is interesting that Sibongile would put things this way. In my analysis of wedding discourse, I have shown that it is what the man wants that is given top priority, followed by the will of the family. Even in the general sermons, the love relationship between a man and a woman is compared to the relationship with Christ. Men, as Christ, are to give love, and women, as the church, are to be submissive. My own personal experience of such sermons, growing up, and the constant reiteration of the need to lose oneself so as to become 'one' with a partner, have informed my decision not to be married. I do not want another 'Christ', and I value the comfort of being 'one' with myself and appreciating the individuality of the people to whom I relate, whether romantically or otherwise. Sibongile believes that I am on a wilful path of my own, but that the Christ-like love of a man will bring me back into submission and happiness. Yet the women's views of submission are more complex, as I discover when speaking to them about marriage relations.

Going 50/50: Definitions of equality and gender roles

The literature on African Pentecostal women suggests that patriarchal structures are entrenched within the sermons, practices and women's groups of their churches. Caroline Tuckey and Louise Kretzschmar (2002) see the Sunday School teachings at the Church of the Province of Southern Africa as a process of socialising girls into a life of inferiority and servitude. Rekopantswe Mate (2002) follows Pentecostal women's groups in Zimbabwe and finds that they are encouraged to take up roles of servitude to men. Their roles are those of caregiver and supporter, and they are expected to submit to their husbands (see also Ellece 2011; KaNdlondlo 2011; Mwaura & Parsitau 2012). Formenism is the term that Sarojini Nadar and Cheryl Potgieter (2010) give to the subscription of Pentecostal women to the superiority of men at their own expense.

I have analysed sermons given by both men and women at Pentecostal churches in Alexandra and found that there is a form of patriarchy encouraged by some preachers. I have also found that some of the sermons contradict the belief in male superiority and that others present 'softer' forms of a patriarchal ideology. But it is the responses and lives of the women to whom these sermons are addressed that my research aims to foreground. Therefore, it is what these women believe, how they understand the different sermons, and the way in which they practise and run their daily lives that I will discuss now. The women all agree that men are the heads of families according to the Bible, but how this headship is taken up is not a simple case of servitude versus dominance. A critique of patriarchy and of any power networks and women's resistance to them is not one that positions women as voiceless and perpetually subjugated victims with no agency. In fact, in the narratives to follow we 'encounter the paradoxical nature of resistance where it simultaneously incorporates both tacit support [for] and rejection [of] various power forms' (Motsemme 2004a: 919).

Magauta works as a helper in Illovo and is divorced. Her idea of male headship is akin to a public play. She sees women as the leaders in their homes, but does not think it is something that should be spoken of aloud: 'A man is a man, he's the head biblically. We cannot override the Word of God. But we are smarter, we head without them knowing. God gives us the wisdom to get men to see things our way.'

Sibongile, a human resources administrator who has been married for six years and has three children, agrees:

> Sivuka si-two ek'seni. Une-stress sakhe sasem-sebenzini, nami ngine-stress sami emsebenzini so 'masifika endlini angicabangi ukuthi kwamele manje ngoba ngingumuntu wesfazane I have to cook and take care of the home while ubaba ehleli esofeni ebukele iTV, uyabona? Yazi neh to tell you the truth i50/50 yenzeka, especially esontweni lethu. Umfundisi he would encourage men to help their wives at home using himself as an example, like he also helps his wife with the dishes. Inkinga ukuthi abafuni legama le 50/50 yilo i-problem but bona they do encourage equality.

> [We both have jobs. He has work stress just as much as I do, so when we get home I don't think that just because I'm a woman I have to cook and take care of the home while the man sits on the couch and watches TV, you see? To tell you the truth, 50/50 does happen, especially at our church. The pastor would encourage men to help their wives at home using himself as an example, like he also helps his wife with the dishes. Their problem is with *hearing* this term '50/50', but they do encourage equality.]

These responses, like many others I received from Alexandra Pentecostal women, problematise the strict binaries presented by the studies on African Pentecostal women and gender ideologies within the Pentecostal church. Magauta, for example, says and believes that the headship of men is stated in the Bible, and she is reluctant to contradict what she calls the 'Word of God', but she does not see herself as inferior or fit to play a subservient role. Where men have been given headship, Magauta sees that women are given wisdom – the wisdom she believes is used by women to have men do what the women want. Sibongile also thinks that women are equal to men. Her response shows that she believes that she contributes as much as her husband to their household, and that she expects him to assist her in roles traditionally assigned to women, like washing the dishes. But she does not tell her husband that they are equal. The problem is in saying '50/50' out loud.

Where Rosinah Mmannana Gabaitse (2015) and Nadar (2010) find Pentecostal hermeneutics to be uncritical of the context in which the Bible was written, and that sermons by preachers apply the patriarchal context of the Bible to the lives of 21st-century women, the words of the women with whom I speak add nuance to these arguments. It may be true that some pastors are literal in their interpretation of the Bible, but the women to whom these sermons are directed do contextualise the text in their own 21st-century, personal ways. Theirs is not a literal application of literal interpretations of biblical texts, but a negotiation of the text to suit their daily needs, all the while avoiding conflict with men and with the discourses of their churches. As reluctant as they are to outwardly use words that contradict biblical texts, they believe in and practise what they consider equality within their homes. Sibongile in fact believes that her own pastor does not assign a domestic role to his wife. I agree to some extent with Nadar and Potgieter that the women's reluctance to be critical of the texts that oppress them is a form of 'patriarchal bargaining' (2010: 147). But this is not done in the cut-and-dried way suggested by these scholars, where women offer servitude in exchange for care from their husbands. Instead, the women are willing to call their husbands the 'heads' in exchange for what they consider equality in the way that household roles are undertaken, and decisions are made. This leads me to a different articulation, offered by Mamphele Ramphele (2000: 115), of silence as negotiation where women 'tread a fine line between affirming the manhood of their men-folk and supporting themselves and their children. The myth of the man as supporter, protector, provider and decision-maker [is] carefully nurtured in an attempt to protect the family and community from moral/ethical breakdown.'

The issue of male headship and female subordination is further problematised with stories such as that of Lucy, a 45-year-old mother of one who has been married for 10 years. Her husband is not Pentecostal. In fact, when they first got married, they both participated in indigenous religious practices, including consulting sangomas and communicating with and making sacrifices for their ancestors. Lucy converted to Pentecostalism without him.

Lucy:

> *Ho bile uncomfortable for ena kabane re kopane re sa kene kereke. It was difficult for ena even le for nna because o-believela ko madlozing* [it was uncomfortable for him because when we met, we both didn't go to church. It was difficult for us both because he believes in ancestral worship]. It was difficult but now I feel like I've conquered something, *nyana* [small]. I had to speak to my husband and explain to him that now I'm born again so I don't do this, and I don't do those *madlozi* [ancestral] things...like that.[22] That's why *ke re* [I say] it was difficult at first because *hape* [also] I was not working. He told me he will stop giving me money since I want to be a *mzalwane* [born again], and I said it's fine God will provide. And I don't know what happened but here we are – I have a job, and when things are happening with their family, they don't invite me coz they know I won't eat food prepared for ancestors. *Ngwana otsamaya le nna kerekeng* [our child attends church with me] and she also doesn't get involved in ancestral worship. Now he understands where I stand. I believe *hore* [that] one day *wa tla mo* [he

> will come here]. I know he will also one day be
> born again; I pray to God for that. My duty as a
> wife is to pray, not force him, and *Modimo* [God]
> will do the rest.

Taking biblical texts literally, or panel-beating Pentecostalism to accommodate African traditional concepts, would mean Lucy leaving the church to follow her husband's beliefs as the head of the household. Or at least allowing her child to take part in the family's ancestral rituals. Instead, Lucy celebrates a small victory which she sees as God's own doing – her husband now accepts her conversion, and she managed to get a job when he tried to use financial abuse to coerce her. Lucy's story is an example of how agency is exerted by these women when they truly believe in something, as she believed in her conversion. Agency is especially exerted even when Lucy knows that she stands to lose the favour of her husband's family – who no longer include her in important traditional rituals.

Lucy does believe in wifely duties, but not in the sense that she occupies an inferior place. She applies her role as wife in prayer, believing that her husband will one day follow her to Charismatic Christianity. Thus, how these women interpret and perform their Pentecostalism is close to Martin Lindhardt's (2015) assessment of Tanzanian Pentecostalism, where a negotiated gender construction allows for a reformed, harmonic private life balanced with power and respectability for men in public. Lindhardt says that Tanzanian Pentecostal men give a public appearance of power and respectability, but aim for a private life of harmony where decisions are taken by themselves and their wives in an equal manner. Jane Soothill (2019) gives attention to a similar contention: that women leaders in the Pentecostal churches of Ghana give a public rhetoric of submission, where their *practices* expose a significant authority within their Pentecostal community. The married Pentecostal women of Alexandra who participated in this study negotiate their place through a public persona of submission, while their private lives are lived out in a more egalitarian manner. It is this interplay between submission and agency that brings about the need to further study the paradox of Pentecostal femininity. Do we call

Pentecostal women oppressed by the discourse of their churches, or liberated by their choosing how to interact with it? Or what if we did neither, instead meeting them as analysts and researchers at the very place of their 'subaltern' voices? Gayatri Chakravorty Spivak (1988) writes about the need to know the voice and the speech acts of the subaltern – as opposed to fitting her, through the violent forces of epistemology, to either the romantic aspects of defending tradition and religion or the so-called liberating aspects of modernity and imperialism. Spivak challenges the woman intellectual to dig deeper into this 'circumscribed task' and not 'disown [it] with a flourish' (1988: 104). Nthabiseng Motsemme (2004a, 2004b) similarly challenges us to consider the symbolism practised by women in silence, prayer and other forms to enrich our interpretive field and lead us to a recognition that 'the mute always speak' (2004a: 910).

In rewriting the story of Bhuvaneswari, Spivak tells the tale of a woman caught between negotiating her patriarchal space and exerting her agency. It is a tragic story about the death of this woman, but not just death by circumstance. Bhuvaneswari ends her life in an act of defiance: by committing suicide during her menstrual cycle. In doing this, she rewrites the script of the illegalised *sati* suicide of her Hindu religion and tradition, all the while answering the patriarchally judgemental questions she knows her family and community will ask of her corpse.

If we consider that 'not only does the will exist, but the existence of the will is required for a subject to be good, or to live in accordance with God's will' (Ahmed 2014b: 60), is Bhuvaneswari then wilful? Are the Pentecostal women with whom I interact wilful too? All seem to be caught within the patriarchal discourses of their communities that render them suicidal in their individuality and wilfulness. Theirs is a voice that whispers loudly between the calls to end patriarchy and their commitment to 'the moral teachings about obedience, love, and humility that have usually buttressed presuppositions about living the Christian life' (Williams 2006: 122).

The voice of the subaltern whispers through the colonised body of femininity. The coloniser of the feminine body is the discourse that asserts that men are powerful and 'heads'. The feminine body is taught the morals of obedience, love and humility. To exist within the colonised space is to coexist, at least in part, with the discourse that renders the feminine speechless. The women do not speak against the interpretations of the biblical text that call them inferior and other. But they do not accept them in practice, either. Theirs is a silent resistance that allows them the claim to a performativity of materialising into acceptable women (see Butler 1988).

Prayer scarves: Respectability and the female fear factory

Earlier in this chapter, I described how the women at Living Waters all took *doeks* and covered their heads and shoulders before the sermon started. I spoke to them to understand why or how this practice came about and what it means to them. To these women, dressing is an expression of their spirituality. They place a lot of importance on dress code relating to their individual relationships with God. Tshego is a 25-year-old woman studying medicine. Her response describes best the sentiments of this group of four women. I will add to this how Sheila, a 34-year-old personal assistant to a senior manager, comments in support of Tshego's views.

Tshego:

> In the church everyone has a prayer scarf. We follow mainly the Jewish side of Christianity, because that's how Christ was – a Jew. So, especially when it comes to women, praying needs to be done with a covered head. As women when we present ourselves to God, we need to cover certain parts of our bodies. Present yourself to God as pure and with no other distractions...The Holy Spirit will let you know personally – it's a personal thing that the Holy Spirit will let you know if you need to cover yourself. Take me for instance with my gift – the prophetic gift is very sensitive, and I know God has actually spoken to me about dress code. I know I cannot come to church wearing shorts, wearing... that sort of stuff. It hinders the flow of the spirit. We present ourselves to God as He would want us to

be, not as we want to be…When you pray, it's in a certain way that makes you, that separates you, that sets you apart from other people. So, if I am in a state of prayer, am I the same as the person on the street?

Sheila:

Mmmhm…sometimes with the covering here [she gestures at her legs], see I may be wearing something long but when I sit it goes up. Then this thing [pointing at her thighs], I am trying to cover it up in respect for the person who is sitting next to or in front of me. It's to maintain the respect. And also, how do you perceive yourself again and it comes to you as a person – how do you present yourself to others. As a child of God especially, you need to be separated, you need to be different from others. Imagine coming here expecting something…can you really expect in a *sgqebezane* [miniskirt] or bum-short to hear from God? The Holy Spirit tells us what to wear but we are rebellious. You won't grasp anything at church.

As I have said, these women relate their dress to their relationship with God and to the levels of their spirituality. Tshego especially highlights this point by telling us how her spiritual gift confines her to a respectable way of dressing. To them, God does not see, hear, or respond to their prayers unless they cover certain parts of their bodies ('can you really expect in a *sgqebezane* to hear from God?'). I use Tamale's (2014) definition of sexuality as a starting point to show how the scarves used at Living Waters are a form of control of women's bodies clothed in respectability.

Tshego and Sheila are examples of how these Pentecostal women's sexuality is intertwined with spirituality, or at least a quest for a spiritual connection with God. This spirituality is dependent not only on the women's self-policing, but also on ensuring that this policing separates them from 'others'. Their relationship with God depends on and is heightened by the women's ability to compare themselves to those who do not maintain the established moralistic rules of sexuality (Tamale

2014, 2016). Failing to uphold these rules, according to these women, entails wearing bum-shorts, miniskirts and dresses that show their shoulders. They believe that if they are to claim the full identity of being the 'child(ren) of God', then they must look different from those who do not lay claim to that identity. They dress to be different from 'someone on the street', and they dress according to instructions that they receive not from their pastors – though the pastor's wife signals the time for *doeks* – but from the Holy Spirit. These women do not present what they practise as personal choices they make, but as instructions received from a higher power – from God.

Yet, though they do stress the importance of an individual relationship with and instruction from God regarding dress code, they also believe that those women who do not comply can be 'led' to this form of respectability.

Sheila:

> But what I like about my church, *neh*?...If you come dressed in an unacceptable way, they will cover you. They will do the covering. They will cover you up with a *doek*. Obviously, there will be some kind of a shame but next time you won't do it...when they do that covering you will feel shame because, walking in, the woman will not feel that she is doing something wrong. Only when they cover you do you see that you are wrong and feel shame. That shame is good because it will be an eye-opener.

Tamale (2016) uses Uganda's miniskirt law to show how the relationship between sexuality and gender affects the choices of those who follow the regulations of respectability and penalises those who do not. She argues that imposing moral codes and laws on womanhood and sexuality eroticises the female body through the control of dress style, and goes on to describe the brutality to which many women in Uganda have been subjected at the hands of local vigilante groups, the police and the courts because they were caught wearing miniskirts. She laments the irony of a law made for the protection of women fuelling violence and violations against women instead. The women at God's Love do not use the physical force detailed by Tamale in her description of the miniskirt law in Uganda, but choose the subtle force of 'shame' to get compliance. Sheila notes that women who come to church in clothing that is deemed 'unacceptable' may not be thinking that they are being erotic or even provocative. These women are obviously not in the kind of conversations with God where the length of their skirts is discussed in relation to spirituality. Sheila is aware of this. But she believes in the duty of a church to come in and 'do the covering' in God's place. Through this act of shaming, the women at God's Love mean to show non-compliant women their wrongs, and then this act of shaming becomes 'an eye-opener'.

Chipo Hungwe (2006) sees respectability and all the performances it entails as women serving patriarchal agendas in order to survive. Binaries are set between a woman deemed respectable and rewarded with 'honour', and an unrespectable woman who is considered perverse and labelled a 'prostitute'. When women are placed in a position to 'survive' the naming and shaming of being on the periphery of society (as 'prostitutes'), it is the very same women who act to 'cover up' those they wish to see in their circle of survival, as Sheila and her fellow women congregants do. These women do not see themselves as being judgemental, or ostracising those who do not cover their bodies in the way expected by the church, but see shaming as a means of teaching survival strategies to women they wish to be a part of their inner group.

Ntsiki is 24 years old, has recently graduated and is now interning at a corporate firm:

> Look, we don't look down on people who dress like that. Like, also we don't look down on prostitutes. But I cannot present myself the same way a prostitute would when she goes to work when I'm coming to church. It's like those are two different women going to different places, but it becomes like those two women are trying to achieve the same things. So, it's very important how we present ourselves.

Tshego:

> I don't see how we can put sex appeal and church in one sentence. For me it just doesn't make sense...*phela* [I mean] not everyone in the church is strong enough to look at it and not feel something and not think of anything. So, the minute a woman comes in wearing a very tight dress, figure-hugging, exposing the back or with slits on the sides, that's a very sexual dress. It has a very sexual picture to it.

So, shaming women whom they see portraying themselves as 'prostitutes' is seen as a means of protection – for those women and for others in the church who are looking at and being distracted by them. I will come back to a discussion of who is distracted later. At this point in the conversation, I was interested in how these women form their own gender identities around the concept of shame. I asked them how and when they had ever felt shamed by others, and if they felt that it had helped them in any way. Lucy has been married for 10 years. She works as an HIV and AIDS treatment counsellor at one of the local clinics.

Lucy:

> With me, the shame was my own. I was wearing a flowing dress and then I was in the spirit and started dancing in the spirit but as I was dancing, I felt something. The dress kept going up, so the spirit left me because now I was thinking about what this dress is doing – it's showing my body. I decided I will never wear that dress again because it disturbed my spirit.

Lucy sees her dress moving and supposedly uncovering her as a disturbance between her and the Holy Spirit. Again, her connection with God is dependent on what she wears, and she feels shame, not because of women in the church showing her she is wrong, but because of a feeling that the spirit is leaving her. If the moral codes of women's fashion exist because of a fear that allowing women to dress as they wish sets female sexuality free, and the female body will come out of 'the tight clutches of patriarchy' (Lutwama-Rukundo 2016: 55), then where does a spiritual element come into play? Where these women see not bodies but the God – the spirit – to whom they choose to submit, does it make them victims of a patriarchal clutch, or does it mean that the 'spirit' is held by and holds them to patriarchy? An understanding of these women as mere victims of a religion that means to hold them to oppressive structures does not do enough to explain how they see themselves to be agents in their practising of this religion, and the confines to which their Pentecostalism restricts them.

Nadar (2005b) suggests that it is not the spirit that holds Pentecostal women to patriarchal practices, but the interpretation of the Bible by Pentecostals. Hence she suggests a move away from a one-dimensional understanding of the spirit. She argues that a multifaceted understanding of the work of the spirit can see women addressing both the physical and the spiritual in a 'more holistic and liberating understanding' (2005b: 367) that can lead to a liberation and empowerment of women.

This framework helps us read Lucy's statement and those given by the other women from God's Love in a slightly different way. If patriarchy has women in its 'clutches' (Lutwama-Rukundo 2016), or keeps them in 'dark and squalid slave-dungeons' (Nadar 2005a: 2), then freeing them from this requires that we see how they may be interpreting their links to the spirit in a way that holds them to this darkness. In other words, I do not mean to read the statements made by these women as proof of their perpetual victimhood, but to understand how their reading of a gendered spirithood holds them to confines that they claim to have chosen, or see as inspired by God.

Nadar (2005b) and Tamale (2014, 2016) see the workings of religion as supported by culture and gender constructions or by the law and culture, respectively. Since these women do not refer to the laws of South Africa when explaining their decision to 'cover up', I will turn to Nadar's linkage, which she calls the 'unholy trinity'. This trinity keeps women oppressed by suggesting that their gendered place in society is already fixed and cannot be changed; and it shows them that an attempt to resist not only stands against their culture but can never be justified within their religion. So, a woman happily dancing in the spirit is always aware of the 'unholy trinity' since she has subscribed to it. She therefore uses that awareness to police herself, see the shame in her dress and align it to a loss of a connection with God.

Speaking further with the women uncovers what I said earlier that I would come to: that the 'unholy trinity' does not only hold them to their relationship with God, but also to a responsibility to the eyes of others – within and outside of the church. You will remember how Tshego alludes to the distraction that is caused by dressing unacceptably. She implies a responsibility placed upon women to think for those who are 'not strong enough'. Sheila is more explicit in her explanation to me of who those people are and why they are 'not strong enough':

> Think of the next person. Think of especially a man! Even the Bible says the weakest point of a man ke hobona skete [is to see a skirt], it's as if that miniskirt is flashing everything. So, you need not be selfish as a woman in church. It's not about you.

The women take this responsibility with them everywhere they go. It is not, but also always is, about them.

Ntsiki:

> I'm always very cautious about my behaviour... we live in a nation where women are victimised brutally...there are things that are happening to women that shouldn't happen. Some of these things are happening because men see images and they meditate on those images. I don't wanna be contributing to that problem – no – I respect and I love my body. So, I dress in a way that others will respect. When I walk in the street and I don't get cat-called I know that's good, I'm dressed in a way that says to men – step back, and they understand – respect!

Sheila:

> I will walk to Bramley right now, but in the back of my mind I'm like, 'God please keep me safe until I get home,' even now in the daylight I ask God to

help me because things happen not only at night.
So, what Ntsiki is saying is true. If you are exposed
as a woman, it's like you are calling the vultures
even more. You are saying 'come!' so that even if
they are very far, they will come running to you to
hurt you. They just see a target.

The gender construction in these statements is clear: men have
the power to hurt women and men are not strong enough to
resist this urge. It becomes the women's own responsibility, then,
to protect themselves by reducing the 'images' that could lead to
their sexual violation by men. Their interpretation of the Bible
cements this responsibilisation, as they believe in a hermeneutic
that justifies men's weakness in 'seeing a skirt'. And even an
attempt to resist this is made impossible in a country that has
elevated gender-based violence to a culture.

These women may be caught in an 'unholy trinity', but similar
experiences of women who may not have the same religious
attachments bond them all together in a 'cult of femininity'.
Pumla Dineo Gqola (2007) uses this term to describe the silence
of abused women, the seeming compliance of women with a
patriarchal system, and the ways in which women repress their
movements in an attempt to protect themselves from gender-
based violence. Gqola further explains how this cult is (re)
produced through rape as an exercise of power:

> The threat of rape is an effective way to remind
> women that they are not safe and that their bodies
> are not entirely theirs. It is an exercise in power
> that communicates that the man creating fear
> has power over the woman who is the target of
> his attention; it also teaches women who witness it
> about their vulnerability either through reminding
> them of their own previous fear or showing them
> that it could happen to them next. It is an effective
> way to keep women in check and often results in
> women curtailing their movement in a physical
> and psychological manner. (Gqola 2017a: 79)

The very product of this male power is what Gqola calls the 'female
fear factory' (2017a: 76–137, 2021). It is the repetition of gender-

based violence that normalises it and places it in the background, making it a part of culture. This constant and repeated action also ensures that fear is manufactured in mass form, rendering all women who will be or are already victims, and those who wish to interrupt the process of this violent production, vulnerable to its dangers. Gqola describes how Nadar's 'unholy trinity' is a product of these women's own fear: 'sometimes these threats of violence are direct and at other times they are translated into regimes that police women and vulnerable others, telling women what body-styling choices are legitimate and which not, shaming people for their body-styling choices, sexual orientation and gender non-conformity' (2017a: 153).

The Holy Spirit is at the centre of Pentecostal practice and interpretation of the Bible. Hence the women at Living Waters believe that it is this same spirit that justifies their fear and the Jewish culture which they use to 'cover' themselves from this fear. The interpretation that Nadar (2005a, 2005b) suggests is one which does not let go of the authority of the spirit in biblical interpretations. Gabaitse says the same thing: that the Holy Spirit is one which offers liberation, true empowerment and transformation, as the 'Holy Spirit is able to cut across discrimination and restrictions imposed by cultures, laws and practices' (2015: 10). It is when this view of the Holy Spirit is taken up by the Pentecostal church that women will begin to enjoy liberation. There are Pentecostal women in Alexandra who agree with this view.

We don't want to be judged

Other Pentecostal women with whom I have spoken do not agree that there is a 'respectable' way to dress. They see these prescriptions as oppressive, and even say that they are against the Bible. Thando, a 32-year-old electrical engineer, and Sibongile, a 34-year-old human resources administrator, were the most vocal about this.

Thando:

> Why is there pressure on us women? Why must we be told what to wear but they don't tell men?

Kushayiwa thina abafazi [we women are always reprimanded], it's very rare that you'll find a pastor *ozoshaya amadoda* [reprimanding men]. It's like *uPastor asho athi 'loyamama loyana babefuna ukum'shaya bathi uyafeba'* [this one pastor once said, 'the woman who was almost beaten because she was caught in an immoral sexual act']²³...*uPastor wathi kodwa ufebe nobani? Iphi lendoda, makashayiwe naye* [the pastor said, 'but with whom was she in this sex act? Where is this man? Let him get beaten too']. So *abantu* [people] always assume that women are the ones in the wrong. It's time the church started training men, it's time. *Phela* [because] women are not raping, beating and committing all sorts of crimes and abuse. It's time they focus on men.

Sibongile:

You know why I left the church I used to go to? One day during the week *ngike ngahlangana nomunye umfundisi and mina ngigqoke i-short, yho lomfundisi wang'beka* [I ran into one of my pastors, and I was wearing shorts. Goodness! The way he looked at me!]. *Sunday mayifika ngathi hayi angiyilapho mina* [the next Sunday I told myself, no, I will not go there] because he will be talking on the pulpit about respectable dress code and *mina* [me] I don't want to be judged. *Futhi* [in fact] nobody wants to be judged, especially based on clothing. We are pushing people away *ngokuba-judgemental thina amakholwa* [by being judgemental, us born agains].

Thando:

Ja mina [yes, me] I've noticed that *labantu aba-judgemental* [these judgemental people] don't even know the Bible, they just speak their own opinions and stories on the pulpit. *Phela* [after all], saying a woman who wears *amaroko namadoek* [dresses and head scarves] is holier than the woman in shorts is not biblical – it's your opinion.

> Mxm [clicks tongue] they don't know the Bible; they
> just want to judge us *ka di-stories le di-opinions tsa
> bone* [with their stories and opinions].

In the respectable dress codes and behaviours they are taught by
Charismatic pastors, the women see sexism. And like Gabaitse
(2015), they vehemently disagree that it can be attributed to the
Bible. Thando cites the violence of men as a concern that pastors
are not only ignoring but pushing onto women. She wants
pastors to start focusing on men and their behaviour instead
of constructing 'holy' women through *doeks* and dresses. These
women are clearly unwilling to accept the fear factory, especially
in their churches, and would rather leave a church that enforces
respectable codes for one that allows them a freedom to choose
how they dress. They see this freedom as their way of living
according to biblical principles and the liberation offered by the
Holy Spirit (Gabaitse 2015).

Dressing is not the only way that these women feel judged and
pushed out by their churches.

Maria:

> This pastor says to me and Mbali, 'since *le na le
> bana* [you have children], you must get married
> to a widower or a man who is divorced'. I almost
> stopped coming to church because how can a
> man of God talk to me like that? He just looks
> down on me because I have children. *Ore nna ke
> etseng ka le* [what does he expect me to do with
> a] return soldier?[24] Huh? I must act desperate to
> marry just any man because *nna* [me] I'm used up
> with children?

Thandaza, a 32-year-old researcher, pursuing her PhD in
chemistry:

> They imply *ukuthi amantombazane* [that girls] are
> the loose sinners who must be helped to stay pure.
> *Manje* [now] the boys are neglected and that's
> why they're messed up. Men *bayinkinga* [are
> problematic], they know nothing about family. It's
> because too much attention is given to us women.

It's like they think *ukuthi umuntu wesfazane uyis'lima kwamele aqeqeshwe and umuntu wes'lisa uright yena udaliwe nje alungile* [that women are stupid and need constant guidance, and men are always right and are created 'right']. *Yithi esithatha i-responsibility mase sinabantwana. Uthole u-brother uyashisa phambili and asazi maybe lo-brother unabantwana abayi-5 but ngeke sazi* [you may find that a 'brother' is on fire in the pulpit and we don't know – maybe that same 'brother' has five children but we will never know] because he doesn't fall pregnant, *angithi* [right]? He can hide the fact that he has children and preach as loud as he likes with no judgement.

The women are aware of the double standards in society and in Pentecostal discourse and practice. Again, their greatest concern is with the sexism that Charismatic pastors tend towards. They attribute the 'problematic nature' of men to sermons and teachings that place the responsibility of correct behaviour on women while allowing men who are irresponsible to carry on with their duties at church with no consequences. These women are rejecting the religions and traditions that place them as deserving recipients of male rage, demanding that they be treated equally to men in their churches, and especially showing that 'Black women also cannot be denied our personal choices, and those choices are becoming increasingly self-assertive and female-oriented' (Lorde 2007: 128).

Pastor fuckboys and the art of dating

One thing that the women at all the churches I visited have in common is their concern with the lack of engagement their pastors have with the dating process. The general feeling amongst these women is that there is a greater focus on celibacy than there is on how to find and identify suitable partners. This has left them vulnerable to being strung along by men, and even being impregnated and left to single motherhood by men who have promised them marriage. They describe the men they meet at church as 'wolves in sheepskin', 'vultures', and more harshly as 'pastor fuckboys'.

Tshego:

> In church there's so much pressure on the men
> that they end up acting like something they're
> not. Brothers now *ba-pusha* [are pushing] towards
> being *moruti* [pastors] so they suppress who
> they really are so that they can give people this
> impression of being holy. That's why most of them
> even when they get married it doesn't even last.
> The wife will be like, 'yho [goodness], this guy
> behind closed doors he is a devil.' They are out
> under this pressure to be the man, the head of the
> house, and told their prayers matter more. It's too
> much for them. It leads to them acting only in the
> way that people want to see them.

Sheila has three children by the same man. When she met him
at church, he represented everything she had thought a good
man should be – God-fearing, kind and loving. The two of them
decided to move in together after some deliberation – and a
promise that he would one day, as soon as he was financially
stable, marry her. Sheila tells me that at the time she felt ready
to start a life with a man and had not had such an opportunity
present itself to her in this way. She thought that her celibate
lifestyle made her appealing to this man, and would ensure that
he valued her virginity and the gift he would receive of being the
one to break it. This is the rest of her story with this man (of
God):

> *Yhoo hayi shem!* [oh no, shame!] Let me tell you,
> *neh*…us women we see things. *Woo*, God help us
> women! We have been through nonsense in life
> and we are still trying…you will be all trying and
> convincing, going all out but really you are only
> pouring water on a stone, hoping it will come to
> life eventually. We bought a house together…a
> month later he got married to another woman.
> A month later…*heh*…we woke up in the same
> house, same bed. He woke up and went to marry
> another woman. Just be careful *aus'* Tumi, there
> are vultures out there. You know when God wants
> to take you out of something, *neh*…it will be bad

> but it's what you need. At that time, I was sick in
> bed, unaware that I'm pregnant. That is love as far
> as ladies are concerned. You will go through bad
> things. Rather wait for God.

Tshego has a similar story to Sheila's. The man who had promised to marry her and had even begun a 'courting' through the church, left both her and that church to marry another woman.[25] In Tshego's case, she blames the church for placing too much pressure on men, leading them to put on an act in exchange for church leadership. Tshego believes that the constant discourse of male headship is just as burdensome to men as it is to women – hence her fiancé leaving her and the church to be with a woman who is not Christian. When I went to visit Tshego at her home, she showed me Facebook pictures of this woman. Tshego pointed out to me in the posts and pictures that this woman had what Tshego did not, 'an outgoing and free personality…that's why he chose her, you see? She is not a stiff little church girl.' She then put the phone down, turned to me and said, '*Aus*' Tumi, our pastors must really be more open to us about dating, if they don't teach us how to date…we're never gonna win.'

But not all the women who have encountered 'pastor fuckboys' see it as a loss of the rare and prized Black man to other women. And though they also do not necessarily 'question the vertical lines of power or authority, nor the sexist assumptions which dictate the terms of that competition' (Lorde 2007: 37), they do recognise a need to have a change in the discourse of their churches. This change, they believe, will better equip them and men in the church for more meaningful and longer-lasting unions.

Tinyiko-Tintswalo, a 25-year-old information technology intern, single, no children, a youth leader:

> I waited till after matric to start dating [rolls eyes]…
> stupid right? He didn't tell me he has a kid. One day
> we were sitting together when his baby momma
> came and dropped a child off. That's the first I
> knew. But I didn't stay because I knew this scene.
> This is exactly what happened to my mother. My
> father's exes just came and dropped their kids off

with my mother. She had to raise all these children that she did not previously know about. I thought, that's not going to happen to me, so I left him. I won't be able to do this.

Femininity from their mothers to their churches

I ended the previous section with Tinyiko's experience because it speaks not only to what the women go through with men in their lives, but also to how they see the potential effects of toxicity through the experiences of their mothers. The church becomes part of a continuum of social, affective and cultural relations. At church, these women find the comfort and relationships that they feel they have missed with their parents and families.

Halala, a 22-year-old BCom student:

> Growing up I always used to feel like, *nna* [me], I'm an embarrassment, like I'm that child she regrets having...because *ke aphapha futhi ke-outspoken* [I am forward and outspoken]. I mean I've always tried to make her see I'm good, like academically I've always done well for her, and...I'd participate in everything at school and get awards, but she'd never celebrate *le nna* [with me]. Now I've accepted that she will be the last person I would talk to if I were to go through something because she's decided that she'll never acknowledge me as good or doing good...So that's why *ke kopile pastor* [I asked my pastor] to help me *ngomshado wami* [organise my wedding], not her...but I pray that I get over this bitterness because I don't want it to affect my children one day.

Lufuno, a 28-year-old unemployed graduate:

> *Ha ke hola ne ke le* [growing up I used to be] free-spirited but then I realised that there were certain topics *tse mama asa bouing ka tsona* [that my mother doesn't discuss]. For instance, when I got my first period, I didn't know what was happening but there wasn't that space *ya hore ke ka hona*

> *ho tla kere* [for me to go and say] this is what's
> happening to me so *ke le ka hlatsoa panty tsa ka
> and then ka lo robala* [I washed my underwear
> and went to bed]. That thing *esa le teng ko heso*
> [is still like that at home]. When it comes to certain
> topics, *ha o tsebe hore oka bua oqala kae* [I have
> no way of talking] coz talking and opening up is
> a huge no-no and I'm like, okay, I might as well
> keep everything to myself. I don't know comfort
> *wabo* [you see], at home there's no such thing.

So, feelings of shame, needing to achieve and to live up to
some form of respectability come with them from their familial
backgrounds. It is their connections with their pastors and
the other women at their churches that cement their existing
beliefs about feminine obligations, but also satisfy their needs
for comfort, open communication, a sense of freedom and
love. Pentecostal church life and participation carry complex
and multifaceted or even contradictory sets of relations and
expectations for these women.

What's love got to do with it?

The women turn to the people they call spiritual mothers and
fathers when they need relationship advice, something they
do not trust their own parents to give them. Tshego was in a
courtship with a man who was lying to her. She told me that
she did not want to listen to her mother's misgivings about that
relationship. She wanted to end what she called the 'curse of single
motherhood', which she had seen through her own upbringing by
a single mother. But luckily, for some of the other women, advice
from their pastors gave them the courage to leave relationships
that were stifling to them.

Sibongile:

> *Ubaba wabantwana bami mangizohlukana
> naye abona naye ukuthi angisafuni, beka like
> emotional[y] blackmail athi kimi, 'Njengoba
> unabantwana abiyi two ubani ozokushada?'
> Beyingihlupha yazi ingihlupha, kodwa bengihamba*

109

ngiye kumshumayeli wami ngimtshele ukuthi yazi ukuya ngami ngifuna ukum'shiya but labantwana laba...Umshumayeli wathi kimi, 'into ekumele uyenze iphuma kuwe uyabona, if you want out then leave. UNkulunkulu won't judge you ngendaba yabantwana instead uzokusiza. UNkulunkulu uzoyenza ukuthi uthole umuntu and then uzoshada.' So, I was freed from that relationship ngendaba yomshumayeli. And ngempela ngamthola umuntu, ngishadile manje.

[The father of my children realised I was going to break up with him, so he would emotionally blackmail me by saying, 'you have two kids now so who will marry you?' That bothered me a lot, so I would go to my Evangelist and tell him that I really want to leave him but the children...The evangelist said, 'you must do what's right for you, if you want out then leave. God won't judge you just because you have children, instead God will help you. God will make sure you find someone, and you will get married.' So, I was freed from that relationship thanks to the Evangelist. I really did find someone, I'm married now.]

Mbali, a 33-year-old finance administrator and mother of one:

I don't know if you will remember Tumi, but *umama wakho uke washumayela lana akhuluma nge-deppression nezinto eziningi* [your mom once preached about depression and some other issues...She was saying] things like, 'some things you can pray for, some things you just need to move away – *phuma lapho!* [let it go!]' *Sjo, Tumi, neh,* that's why *ngithi* [I say] I thank God, because after that message *yho!* I am so free coz by God's grace, *ngathi yazini,* [I told myself that] I am cutting ties. *Ngamtshela ukuthi yazi baba umntwana wakho uzombona mara uzo-phone ule egate, angikufuni endlini yami* [so I told the father of my child that he can see his son, but he must call first, he can no longer come into my house]. I no longer want him in my space.

Pentecostal women also turn to each other for emotional support. Frahm-Arp (2015a) finds that women's networks within Pentecostal churches perform a surveillance that renders women helpless and unable to end relationships with men who hurt them. My sense of the Pentecostal Charismatic churches in Alexandra that I have researched is that the women build networks that allow them to have honest and open conversations with each other, be it about abuse, emotional issues with spouses, or problems within their families.

Tumelo, a 47-year-old administrator of a local NGO, 2 children, divorced:

> *Yazi neh*, to tell you the truth…I would have stayed with my ex if I didn't talk. Maybe I would be dead like *usis* 'Thami.[26] But it was one day long ago, *siku* [we were at] prayer, *neh,* and uPastor said something *nge* [about] silence, she said 'it will kill you', and I just started crying. The women prayed for me and after one of them called me and said she will help me if I want to leave him – like she knew what he was doing. *Yazi* I left, even uPastor supported me. I left him and I never looked back.

Mathero, a 36-year-old database administrator:

> *Go bua nnete* [the truth is] we live in a time when failure is not allowed. We can't admit that we have failed at marriage, at relationships or anything because Christianity now doesn't allow us our human flaws. *Ha re ho ne hoba batho* [we can't be human]. But I thank God for these women because they allowed me to cry, they didn't judge me when my brother *aya kotronkong* [was arrested]. It's not easy telling people that you have a family member *ko jele* [in jail]…but I told them, and they continue to pray with me and give me strength.

These are women who, even in their differences, have found a sisterhood that lifts them and gives them hope for their future. They open up to each other about the struggles they face, and in this opening up to others they see themselves overcoming difficulties too. I imagine this sisterhood within the Charismatic Christian setting in Alexandra to be one that almost touches on the sisterhood described by Gqola (2017a) and Lorde (2007). Almost. Almost, because there is still some way to go.

Conclusion

Alexandra township is filled with all sorts of life and culture on a weekend. With all the choices open to them, all the women I speak to choose to spend their Sundays at church. When they are given rules about how to dress and present themselves, when they are told to be subservient to men, they choose to stay in church. It is this choice, and their negotiation of how they apply their churches' prescriptions to their femininity, that this chapter has uncovered.

I have found that the constructions of femininity vary with the pastors, sermons and services I have attended. Applying binaries between the men and the women pastors is not an easy task. I cannot just flippantly state that the men are patriarchal and the women liberatory in their speech acts – even though the sermons that are more 'radical' in the way of feminising the church and its congregants were delivered by women pastors, Xoli and Fuzeka. Soft patriarchy is evident in the poem that celebrates women which I cite earlier in this chapter, and in some of the sermons given by both men and women, where femininity is embodied in normative ways that direct women towards tradition and restrict them to ideas that deny freedom. The pastors also employ strategies of concealment that address women and some of the choices they make without considering the power relations between men and women that make it difficult for women to do or act otherwise. Assuming women's autonomy is no way to break through the boundaries within which they find themselves, especially when these very boundaries are reproduced through the discourses of male headship as a natural state created by a male God.

There are instances, however, when the sermons show that these pastors have an intention to break through some of these boundaries. Pastor Nyathi expresses his desire to have women in leadership regardless of their marital status. Pastor Fuzeka uses feminised metaphors to give a descriptive narrative of God – I imagine for a moment the change of imagery which could give us a God(dess) that does not aim to violently subjugate and dominate. What a difference that would make for gender constructs and relations in our society. And Pastor Xoli does what some of the women in this study wish could be done more often: she addresses men and calls for them to not only change their behaviour but do so in a way that emulates the so often mocked emotional attachments of women.

How far and how often any of these sometimes conflicting and complex discourses of the four pastors are embraced by the women I speak with becomes another site of contestation and paradox. For there are times when they seem to resist oppressive discourses, especially when they feel that these discourses do not fit their daily lives. But there are also times when the discourses of the sermons are taken up by these women without question. The desire for marriage, for example, is one that all the women at all of the churches I have visited regard as natural to every woman – without any regard to any person who does not conform to their idea of gendered differences, or even to cis-gender women like themselves who believe in a different life choice. Theirs is a rigidly heteronormative construction of the happiness that God intends for women – to be unified in marriage with men. However, the naturalised state of men, women and their roles becomes complicated when we come to discuss equality in relationships and marriage. In this case, I discover that the women are only willing to accept the idea of male headship through lip-service, but expect to be included in all household decisions and have their men assist them with 'feminine' duties.

Another issue of contestation comes with discussions of respectability. Not all women agree that there is a respectable form of conduct or dress to which they should adhere. Some women question the sexism in such discourses and insist that the prescriptions given to them should be given to men as much as, if not more than, to them. On the other hand, the women who agree to maintain respectable 'standards' reveal to me how their scarves and long dresses only serve to protect them from the violence of men. They believe that any inappropriate advances, comments and outright ferocity they may experience at the hands of men are only as a result of their own failing to uphold a respectable femininity. Remarkably, all the women on either side of these beliefs cite spirituality, a relationship with God and knowledge of the Bible as the main motivators of their opposing stances.

It is not only the church or sermons that influence the decisions these women make, however. Speaking with them reveals how their familial backgrounds and especially relationships with their mothers give rise to their views on certain matters. Some of the women have turned to and keep holding to their churches and their pastors to fill voids that have been left by strained relationships with their own families. Sometimes these strains seem to spill into relationships they try to build with potential spouses. But it is also through their churches and their pastors that some of the women believe that they have been freed from toxic relationships with men. Several of them attribute their decisions to brave single motherhood to advice received from pastors who do not judge them, but give them hope through prayer for more suitable partners.

Finally, the Charismatic women of Alexandra township build strong bonds with each other. When they tell their stories to me in groups, I catch glimpses of familiarity in the other women, which suggests that they have heard the accounts before. They believe that God has placed them together to be sisters – in prayer, advice, general life choices, celebrations, parenthood and happiness. In each other, they find what they search for – a God who loves, validates, listens, sees and wants their happiness and success.

Chapter 6

A question of difference

> I urge each one of us here to reach down into that deep place of knowledge inside herself and touch that terror and loathing of any difference that lives there. See whose face it wears. Then the personal as the political can begin to illuminate all our choices.
>
> — Audre Lorde, *Sister Outsider* (2007: 74)

Audre Lorde identifies three ways that difference is handled: ignore it, emulate it if it is dominant, or destroy it if it is subordinate. Lorde ascribes this fear and hatred of difference to a mechanism programmed into each of us as members of profit economies that aim to and need to have outsiders as surplus. Difference is thus misnamed and misused as a means to produce prejudice and confusion.

When difference is denied, research of Black subjects is distorted by white positionalities and brings those subjects into our view in reduced forms. When difference is denied, we see it only in the form of white anthropologists' recollections of the difficulty of entering a field because the communities researched and their leaders were apprehensive, cagey or defensive. It is the denial of difference that refuses to know and see what would make the Black subject reluctant to be placed under anthropological scrutiny. And it is the denial of difference that shows us the reasons these subjects are right to be disconcerted by the white gaze.

My study uncovers difference in its constructions, clothed in Black femininity. Difference in these cases is also a site of polarisation and of binaries that teach women to reject some things and embrace others in pursuit of 'proper' Christianity and spirituality. Femininity is thus presented in sermons as a challenge to the women congregants to set themselves apart. To attain recognition as the proper and the respectable, women are to imitate dominant forms of a spiritual femininity constructed by their pastors' discourses. They are to be humble, beautiful servants of God, men and children. They are to attain a conditional happiness through silent elation as the passive recipients of male advances. Women are also to be heterosexual, childbearing, nurturing, and if not married at least marriage-worthy. Women who do this are 'proper' Christians, and those who fail at it are not. Even the women pastors, who are more radically egalitarian in their sermons, at times fall back into this hegemonic construction of difference. To them, the Christian and the blessed woman does not succumb to sexual advances made by a man more powerful than her. The blessed woman resists even if it may lead to her starvation. Such strong and moral women are considered more respectable and worthy of honour by the women pastors, who also promise them God's rewards.

Pentecostal women go about adopting some of these markers of proper Christianity and creating their own, too. When difference is denied, heteronormativity takes on the role of correcting the one who is different. No alternative possibilities can be seen in the one who does not share the 'natural' desires of the other women. Rejecting the different, they will rather convince me that there is no difference, that it is time-based, it will lapse, and soon I will realise that just like them and like any other woman, I desire the natural heterosexual happiness that can only be provided by a union, in marriage, with a man. When difference is loathed, and the one who is different is seen as inferior, shame becomes the corrector.

Some of the women admit to shaming those who do not conform to a respectable dress code at church. They see the shame as an eye-opener and a challenge that will bring the deviant closer to God. Spiritual women are different, and the non-spiritual can be made that way once they are shamed: shamed into covering up, shamed into an awakened spirituality. You're welcome. But to be different is also to stand apart from the rapeable. Difference is a tool that operates with the violence of patriarchy, proving that these women comply, showing the master that there is no need to punish them. They are different from the other slaves. They are, or should be, unrapeable. Yet they still live in fear.

Difference makes these women marriable, but also playable by the men they hope to marry. They want to be different from the girls on the street, but those girls are not 'church' and they are not boring. They want the men to see them as different and reward them for their difference: marry them for the difference. When women are placed as rivals of each other and accept that placement, it is only to manage and uphold a male supremacist ideology. This rivalry can be clothed as beauty, respectability, honourable conduct and heightened spirituality. But it is rivalry: a competition between women who only see their value when it is acknowledged through the sexist assumptions that construct the terms of this value.

Difference then becomes a tool of patriarchy that sifts the worthy women from the deviant so that the deviant can become part of the surplus – the usable, ungrievable, disposable. And to survive, women urge themselves on to reach a place of worth by drawing lines of difference that place them apart from their binary opposites. It is exhausting, they know, because in a profit economy no one is irreplaceable, and what was considered worthy and 'proper' yesterday might not be so tomorrow. But survival is just that. Survival does not require one to question and undo unjust and violent structures of power. It only requires one to outdo the next woman. Outdoing her, showing her up for loathable difference, is enough to buy the time for a comfortable placing in misogynoir, temporary as it may be. And when stories of victory achieved by women who successfully fought off abusive men become the feminised markers of strong versus weak women, that victory is annulled.

We must begin to see the oppression that comes from outside when it roots itself within. We must realise that freedom is not found in the crumbs that patriarchy, racism and heterosexism leave for us to bicker over in our oppressed corners. Borrowing the face of the oppressor to oppress myself further can never free me, for 'the master's tools will never dismantle the master's house' (Lorde 2007: 74).

Alexandra's Pentecostal women are learning to throw out these tools. A difference is forged in imageries of a femme God. They have an unease with discourses that call them inferior and 'other'. When they see women who have been 'othered' by the codes of respectability, they reject a spirithood that is based on what they wear and the number of children they have. Instead, they seek for and embrace one that gives them the courage to walk away when they are stifled or abused; or to stand their ground with the 'heads' of their families and establish their own headship. Together, or with the help of their pastors, these women refuse to die in silence. They reach out to each other openly and honestly for courage and for hope.

They come into churches searching for a God and a spirithood that sees them for all they are and all they are not. In the spirithood they hold so fast to are their struggles and their triumphs and whatever may lie in between. It is within these cracks that they come to a different connectedness, family, bond: ties with people you could otherwise have not met or been friends with; bonding through the holding of hands in prayer; seeing yourself in the testimony of a spiritual sister. These are the results of a difference that is embraced.

So, the unlearning of internalised oppression is possible. To see a value in ourselves that is not mirrored in the eye of the master is doable. And to question and dismantle the structures that hurt society and permeate our very being is imperative. Then the sisterhood that is already evident and already budding can bloom. Our sisterhood can burst into colours of power and move us from the margins to the centre – in the name of a sisterhood and all its possibilities.

If I were to write a personal love note to my Pentecostal sisters, it would begin with Audre Lorde and end with bell hooks: 'in our world divide and conquer must become define and empower' (Lorde 2007: 75); and at every turn, when the voice of the oppressor beckons, turn again to a true and firm sisterhood to uproot the loathing of difference. Finally, always remember that 'feminism is for everybody' (bell hooks 2000).

About the author

Tumi Mampane is an African feminist PhD candidate in the Department of Communication and Media, University of Johannesburg, affiliated to the NRF SARChi Chair in African Feminist Imagination at Nelson Mandela University. She is also a lecturer in the Department of Communication Science, University of the Free State. Her research interests include cultural and media studies, township femininities, popular culture, African Pentecostalisms, discourse analysis, narrative analysis, ethnography and feminist theory.

Photo gallery

Figure P1. Bishop Silawuli and Pastor Thoko (my mother).
Source: God's Love Christian Family Church Facebook page, https://web.facebook.com/photo/?fbid=3324435580915796&set=pb.100064414820623.-2207520000, accessed 22 October 2022.

Figure P2. Pastor Patrick and his wife Mrs Sexoka, Nkuli in the background.
Source: God's Love Christian Family Church Facebook page, https://web.facebook.com/photo/?fbid=3324435580915796&set=pb.100064414820623.-2207520000, accessed 22 October 2022.

Figure P3. Nkuli leading worship at Thusong Youth Centre.

Source: The author.

Figure P4. Phutaditjaba Community Centre and a young, unnamed beneficiary.

Source: The author.

Figure P5. Ko Bareng (The Bar).

Source: The author.

Figure P6. Ko Bareng patrons (left–right): Mahlangu, John Namane and John Masangu.

Source: The author.

Figure P7. One of Alexandra's oldest homes.

Source: The author.

Figure P8. Another 'old home' in Alexandra, protected by a wall.

Source: The author.

Figure P9. 15th Avenue on Hofmeyr Street, Alexandra.

Source: The author.

Figure P10. The Roosevelt Street entrance to Pan Africa, Alexandra. Pan Africa is the hub of Alexandra's businesses, which include supermarkets, malls and street vendors. The Alexandra Magistrate Court and Department of Home Affairs branch are also found here.

Source: The author.

Notes

1   Pastor Xoli's name and the name of her church have been anonymised at her request.

2   The Acts in question were the Natives (Urban Areas) Act (No. 21 of 1923), the Native Trust and Land Act (No. 18 of 1936), the Native (Urban Areas) Consolidation Act (No. 25 of 1945), the Group Areas Act (No. 41 of 1950) and the Prevention of Illegal Squatting Act (No. 52 of 1951).

3   The original spelling of this name in the Bible is Gomorrah. I have chosen to use the spelling widely accepted in popular culture, and used in the new series on the television channel Mzansi Magic that is set in Alexandra township. See https://www.dstv.com/mzansimagic/en-za/show/gomora, accessed 5 November 2022.

4   The mainline churches are the more 'traditional' and 'long-established' churches; they include the Anglican, Methodist and Catholic churches.

5   See also Van Wyk I, A look at the 'prosperity gospel' in South Africa. *CNBC Africa*, 25 February 2019. Accessed 16 May 2019, https://www.cnbcafrica. com/special-report/2019/02/25/a-look-at-the-prosperity-gospel-in-south-africa/; Zulu A, Huge church accused of scamming members, *Mail & Guardian*, 22 February 2019. Accessed 16 May 2019, https://mg.co.za/ article/2019-02-22-00-theprosperity-gospelmeans-exploitation/.

6   LGBTQI+ refers to people who identify as lesbian, gay, bisexual, transgender, queer or intersex.

7   The church leaders' response was given in a press release on 22 October 2005, 'Press release: The UCKG's statement on Ilana van Wyk's book'. See https://web.archive.org/web/20160221184108/http://www.uckg.org. za/news/press-release-the-uckgs-statement-on-ilana-van-wyks-book/, accessed 2 January 2023.

8   Mshoza is a South African musician and dancer who represents, to South African pop culture consumers, the essence of township women. She is fun, unapologetically loud and hardly speaks English. *BoMshoza* is now a widely used descriptor for women who are just as loud, and considered 'unsophisticated'.

9   Allan Anderson writes about Pentecostalism as a researcher and member/ co-pastor of a Charismatic church in Soshanguve, a township near the city of Tshwane.

10 See also Mupotsa D, Lobola for my love. *Mail & Guardian*, 18 July 2008. Accessed 16 May 2019, https://www.pressreader.com/south-africa/mail-gu ardian/20080718/282007553163761.

11 PK is the 'endearing' term for all whose parents are ordained or practising pastors.

12 See Mayekiso (1996) on housing development and the creation of the so-called Black middle class in the 1980s.

13 *Bazalwane* is a popular way of referring to Pentecostals.

14 *Zozo* huts are small houses made of corrugated sheeting. These are common in most South African townships but were specifically brought

into Alexandra during the late 1980s to early 1990s as temporary homes for families who were displaced by the ongoing Inkatha attacks. Most of these families were not able to get their homes back after the transition to democracy.

15 This is a hymn referencing Peter's visit to Cornelius in Acts 10:33: 'and it was good of you to come. All of us are here now in the presence of God to listen to everything the Lord has ordered you to say.'

16 Evangelising is done to convince people outside of the church to not only convert to Born Again Christianity but join the church as well.

17 Revelations 12:11: 'They have conquered him by the blood of the Lamb and the word of their testimony.'

18 Mupotsa D, Lobola for my love. *Mail & Guardian*, 18 July 2008. Accessed 16 May 2019, https://www.pressreader.com/south-africa/mail-guardian/20080718/282007553163761

19 This statement follows a reading from Proverbs 4:23: 'Above all else, guard your heart, for everything you do flows from it.'

20 Shonda Rhimes, *Scandal*, 2012–2018, Disney–ABC Domestic Television.

21 For '50/50' see https://www.youtube.com/watch?v=fIKQh4t8F8k; for 'Independent Women' see https://www.youtube.com/watch?v=0lPQZni7I18.

22 Conversion to Pentecostalism, a monolithic religion, is considered a rejection of indigenous African practices. Pentecostals are mostly warned against worshipping or communicating with ancestors as it is a practice believed to contradict the omnipresent power of God.

23 Thando refers here to a Bible verse, John 8:3–11, about a woman who was caught in the act of adultery and almost stoned according to the Law of Moses, but Jesus stopped this from happening.

24 A 'return soldier' is a colloquial term used in the township to describe a person whose marriage has failed and who is now 'returning' to a life of singlehood.

25 Courting is the dating process of Charismatic Christians. When young members of a church declare their interest in each other, the leaders of the church allow them to date but mostly under strict supervision, to ensure that they do not break the celibacy codes and that their main aim is to get married. (See Frahm-Arp 2012; Parsitau 2009; Pearce 2012; Quiroz 2016.)

26 Thami is a woman who was murdered by her husband in 2013. I have changed her name to maintain anonymity.

References

Adogame A (2008) To God be the glory. *Critical Interventions* 2(3–4): 147–159

Ahmed S (2010) *The promise of happiness.* Durham, NC: Duke University Press

Ahmed S (2014a) *The cultural politics of emotion* (2nd ed.). Edinburgh: Edinburgh University Press

Ahmed S (2014b) *Willful subjects.* Durham, NC: Duke University Press

Ahmed S (2017) *Living a feminist life.* Durham, NC: Duke University Press

Anderson A (2002) The newer Pentecostal and Charismatic churches: The shape of future Christianity in Africa? *Pneuma* 24(2): 167–184

Anderson A (2013) *An introduction to Pentecostalism: Global Charismatic Christianity* (2nd ed.). Cambridge: Cambridge University Press

Anderson A (2018) *Spirit-filled world, religious dis/continuity in African Pentecostalism.* Cham: Springer

Anderson AH (2005) New African initiated Pentecostalism and Charismatics in South Africa. *Journal of Religion in Africa* 35(1): 66–93

Anderson A & Otwang S (1993) *Tumelo: The faith of African Pentecostals in South Africa.* Pretoria: University of South Africa

Argyle M (2000) *Psychology and religion.* London: Routledge

Asamoah-Gyadu JK (2005) Of faith and visual alertness: The message of 'mediatized' religion in an African Pentecostal context. *Material Religion* 1(3): 336–356

Asamoah-Gyadu JK (2007a) Broken calabashes and covenants of fruitfulness: Cursing barrenness in contemporary African Christianity. *Journal of Religion in Africa* 37: 437–460

Asamoah-Gyadu JK (2007b) 'Get on the internet!' says the LORD: Religion, cyberspace and Christianity in contemporary Africa. *Studies in World Christianity* 13(3): 225–242

Asamoah-Gyadu JK (2015) Prosperity and poverty in the Bible: Search for balance. Accessed 25 August 2020, https://www. lausanne.org/content/prosperity-and-poverty-in-the-bible-search-for-balance

Bailey J (2008) First steps in qualitative data analysis: Transcribing. *Family Practice* 25(2): 127–131

Baloyi EM (2008a) Patriarchal structures, a hindrance to women's rights. PhD thesis, University of Pretoria

Baloyi EM (2008b) The biblical exegesis of headship: A challenge to patriarchal understanding that impinges on women's rights in the church and society. *Verbum et Ecclesia* 29(1): 1–13

Baloyi EM (2010) An African view of women as sexual objects as a concern for gender equality: A critical study. *Verbum et Ecclesia* 31(1): 1–6

Barfoot C & Sheppard G (1980) Prophetic vs. priestly: The changing role of women clergy in classical Pentecostal churches. *Review of Religious Research* 22(1): 2–17

Benya F (2018) Commodification of the Gospel and the socio-economics of neo-Pentecostal/Charismatic Christianity in Ghana. *Legon Journal of the Humanities* 29(2): 116–146

Berger PL (2008) *Faith and development: A global perspective.* Johannesburg: Centre for Development and Enterprise

Bernstein A & Rule S (2010) Flying under the South African radar: The growth and impact of Pentecostals in a developing country. In PL Berger & G Redding (Eds) *The hidden form of capital: Spiritual influences in societal progress.* London: Anthem Press

Bishau D (2013) The prosperity gospel: An investigation into its pros and cons with examples drawn from Zimbabwe. *International Open & Distance Learning Journal* 1(1): 65–75

Bompani B & Brown T (2015) A 'religious revolution'? Print media, sexuality, and religious discourse in Uganda. *Journal of Eastern African Studies* 9(1): 110–126

Bonner PL & Nieftagodien N (2008) *Alexandra: A history.* Johannesburg: Wits University Press

Brown-Vincent LD (2019) Seeing it for wearing it: Autoethnography as Black feminist methodology. *Taboo: The Journal of Culture and Education* 18(1): 108–125

Brusco E (1986) Colombian evangelism as a strategic form of women's collective action. *Feminist Issues* 6: 3–13

Brusco E (2010) *The reformation of machismo: Evangelical conversion and gender in Colombia.* Austin: University of Texas Press

Burchardt M (2018) Saved from hegemonic masculinity? Charismatic Christianity and men's responsibilization in South Africa. *Current Sociology* 66(1): 110–127

Burdick J (1990) Gossip and secrecy: Articulation of domestic conflict in three different regions of urban Brazil. *Sociological Analysis* 50(2): 153–170

Butler J (1988) Performative acts and gender constitution: An essay in phenomenology and feminist theory. *Theatre Journal* 40(4): 519–531

Butler J (1990) *Gender trouble: Feminism and the subversion of identity.* New York: Routledge

Butler J (1993) *Bodies that matter: On the discursive limits of 'sex'.* London: Routledge

Butler J (2004) *Undoing gender.* London: Routledge

Casselberry JS (2008) 'Blessed assurance': Belief and power among African American Apostolic women. PhD thesis, Yale University

Casselberry J & Pritchard EA (Eds) (2019) *Spirit on the move: Black women and Pentecostalism in Africa and the diaspora.* Durham, NC: Duke University Press

Cazarin R & Griera M (2018) Born a pastor, being a woman: Biographical accounts on gendered religious gifts in the diaspora. *Culture and Religion* 19(4): 451–470

CDE South Africa (2008) Under the radar: Pentecostalism in South Africa and its potential social and economic role. Accessed 10 February 2020, https://www.cde.org.za/under-the-radar-pentecostalism-in-south-africa-and-its-potential-social-and-economic-role/

Chesnut RA (1997) *Born again in Brazil: The Pentecostal boom and the pathogens of poverty*. New Brunswick, NJ: Rutgers University Press

Chesnut RA (2012) Prosperous prosperity: Why the health and wealth gospel is booming across the globe. In K Attanasi & A Yong (Eds) *Pentecostalism and prosperity*. New York: Palgrave Macmillan

Chitando E & Biri K (2013) 'Faithful men of a faithful God'? Masculinities in the Zimbabwe Assemblies of God Africa. *Exchange* 42: 34–50

Claffey P (2007) *Christian churches in Dahomey-Benin: A study of the socio-political role*. Leiden: Brill

Coleman S (2000) *The globalisation of Charismatic Christianity: Spreading the gospel of prosperity*. Cambridge: Cambridge University Press

Coleman S (2011) Prosperity unbound? Debating the 'sacrificial economy'. *The Economics of Religion: Anthropological Approaches Research in Economic Anthropology* 31: 23–45

Collins P (2000) *Black feminist thought: Knowledge, consciousness, and the politics of empowerment* (2nd ed.). London: Routledge

Comaroff J & Comaroff JL (1999) Occult economies and the violence of abstraction: Notes from the South African postcolony. *American Ethnologist* 26(2): 279–303

Corten A & Marshall-Fratani R (Eds) (2001) *Between Babel and Pentecost: Transnational Pentecostalism in Africa and Latin America*. Bloomington, IN: Indiana University Press

Crawley AT (2008) Let's get it on! Performance theory and Black pentecostalism. *Black Theology: An International Journal* 6(3): 308–329

Crenshaw K (1989) Demarginalizing the intersection of race and sex: A Black feminist critique of antidiscrimination doctrine, feminist theory and antiracist politics. *University of Chicago Legal Forum* 8(1): 139–167

Czeglédy AP (2008) A new Christianity for a new South Africa: Charismatic Christians and the post-apartheid order. *Journal of Religion in Africa* 38: 284–311

Daly M (1985) *Beyond God the father: Toward a philosophy of women's liberation* (2nd ed.). Boston: Beacon Press

Dangarembga T (2006) *The book of not*. Oxfordshire: Ayebia Clarke Publishing

Davies A (2003) *The native speaker: Myth and reality*. Clevedon: Multilingual Matters

Davies B, Browne J & Petersen EB (2004) The ambivalent practices of reflexivity. *Qualitative Inquiry* 10(3): 360–389

Deacon G & Lynch G (2013) Allowing Satan in? Moving toward a political economy of neo-Pentecostalism in Kenya. *Journal of Religion in Africa* 43: 108–130

De Beauvoir S (2010) *The second sex*. English translation by C Borde and S Malovany-Chevallier. New York: Vintage

De Fina A (2015) Narrative and identities. In A De Fina & A Georgakopoulou (Eds) *The handbook of narrative analysis*. Chichester: John Wiley & Sons

De Lima Costa C & Alvarez SE (2014) Dislocating the sign: Toward a translocal feminist politics of translation. *Signs: Journal of Women in Culture and Society* 39(3): 557–564

De Witte M (2003) Altar Media's living word: Televised Charismatic Christianity in Ghana. *Journal of Religion in Africa* 33(2): 172–203

129

De Witte M (2011) Business of the Spirit: Ghanaian broadcast media and the commercial exploitation of Pentecostalism. *Journal of African Media Studies* 3(2): 189–204

Dictionary Unit for South African English (2011) *Oxford South African concise dictionary* (2nd ed.). Oxford: Oxford University Press.

Dillard CB (2000) The substance of things hoped for, the evidence of things not seen: Examining an endarkened feminist epistemology in educational research and leadership. *Qualitative Studies in Education* 13(6): 661–681

Dillard CB (2003) Cut to heal, not to bleed: A response to Handel Wright's 'An endarkened feminist epistemology?' Identity, difference and the politics of representation in educational research. *International Journal of Qualitative Studies in Education* 16(2): 227–232

Dosekun S (2016) The politics of fashion and beauty in Africa. *Feminist Africa* 21: 1–6

Dube EE (2019) Desperation in an attempt to curb modern-day prophets: Pentecostalisation and the church in South Africa and Zimbabwe. *Journal of the South African Theological Seminary* 27: 25–35

Dube M (2007) God never opened the Bible to me: The role of women in Botswana churches. In F Nkomazana (Ed.) *Church history of Botswana*. Pietermaritzburg: Cluster

Dube M (2014) Between the spirit and the word: Reading the gendered African Pentecostal Bible. *Hervormde Teologiese Studies* 70(1): 1–7

Ellece S (2011) 'Be a fool like me': Gender construction in the marriage ceremonies in Botswana – a critical discourse analysis. *Agenda* 25(1): 43–52

Engelke M (2004) Discontinuity and the discourse of conversion. *Journal of Religion in Africa* 34(1–2): 82–109

Engelke M (2010) Past Pentecostalism: Notes on rupture, realignment, and everyday life in Pentecostal and African independent churches. *Africa* 80(2): 177–199

Eriksen A (2014) Sarah's sinfulness: Egalitarianism, denied difference, and gender in Pentecostal Christianity. *Current Anthropology* 55(10): 262–270

Fairclough N (2003) *Analysing discourse*. London: Routledge

Frahm-Arp M (2010) *Professional women in South African Pentecostal Charismatic churches*. Boston: Brill

Frahm-Arp M (2012) Singleness, sexuality, and the dream of marriage. *Journal of Religion in Africa* 42: 369–383

Frahm-Arp M (2015a) Surveillance and violence against women in Grace Bible Church and the Zionist Christian Church. *Journal of Gender and Religion in Africa* 21(1): 71–84

Frahm-Arp M (2015b) The political rhetoric in sermons and select social media in three Pentecostal Charismatic evangelical churches leading up to the 2014 South African election. *Journal for the Study of Religion* 28(1): 115–141

Frahm-Arp M (2016) Constructions of mothering in Pentecostal Charismatic churches. *Neotestamentica* 50(1): 145–163

Freeman D (Ed.) (2012) *Pentecostalism and development: Churches, NGOs and social change in Africa*. New York: Palgrave Macmillan

Gabaitse RM (2012) Towards an African Pentecostal feminist biblical hermeneutic of liberation: Interpreting Acts 2:1–47 in the context of

Botswana. PhD thesis, University of KwaZulu-Natal

Gabaitse RM (2015) Pentecostal hermeneutics and the marginalisation of women. *Scriptura* 114(1): 1–12

Gbote EZ & Kgatla ST (2014) Prosperity gospel: A missiological assessment. *HTS Theological Studies* 70(1): 1–10

Gibson WJ & Brown A (2009) *Working with qualitative data.* London: Sage

Gifford P (1990) Prosperity: A new and foreign element in African Christianity. *Religion* 20(4): 373–388

Gifford P (2007). Expecting miracles: The prosperity gospel in Africa. Accessed 25 August 2020, https://www.christiancentury.org/article/2007-07/expecting-miracles-0

Gilbert J (2015) The heart as a compass: Preaching self-worth and success to single young women in a Nigerian Pentecostal church. *Journal of Religion in Africa* 45: 307–333

Gqola PD (2001) Ufanele uqavile: Blackwomen, feminisms and postcoloniality in Africa. *Agenda* 16(50): 11–22

Gqola PD (2007) How the 'cult of femininity' and violent masculinities support endemic gender-based violence in contemporary South Africa. *African Identities* 5(1): 111–124

Gqola PD (2017a) *Rape: A South African nightmare.* Johannesburg: MFBooks

Gqola PD (2017b) *Reflecting rogue: Inside the mind of a feminist.* Johannesburg: MFBooks

Gqola PD (2021) *Female fear factory: Gender and patriarchy under racial capitalism.* Johannesburg: MFBooks

Grant J (2004) Black theology and the Black woman. In J Bobo, C Hudley & C Michel (Eds) *The black studies reader.* New York: Routledge

Hackett RI (1998) Charismatic/Pentecostal appropriation of media technologies in Nigeria and Ghana. *Journal of Religion in Africa* 28(3): 258–278

Hackett RI (2009) The new virtual (inter)face of African Pentecostalism. *Society* 46: 496–503

Hackman M (2018) *Desire work: Ex-gay and Pentecostal masculinity in South Africa.* Durham, NC: Duke University Press

Harding SG (Ed.) (2004) *The feminist standpoint theory reader: Intellectual and political controversies.* New York: Routledge

Hasu P (2006) World Bank & heavenly bank in poverty & prosperity: The case of Tanzanian Faith Gospel 1. *Review of African Political Economy* 33(110): 679–692

Haynes N (2012) Pentecostalism and the morality of money: Prosperity, inequality, and religious sociality on the Zambian Copperbelt. *Journal of the Royal Anthropological Institute* 18: 123–139

Haynes N (2018) Why can't a pastor be president of a 'Christian nation'? Pentecostal politics as religious mediation. *PoLAR: Political and Legal Anthropology Review* 41(1): 60–74

Hendricks S (2019) Prosperity gospel a problem in Africa Chitwood says. Accessed 16 May 2019, http://www.bpnews.net/52705/prosperity-gospel-a-problem-in-africa-chitwood-says

Heuser A (2016) Charting African prosperity gospel economies. *HTS Theological Studies* 72(3): 1–10

Hodgson DL (Ed.) (2001) *Gendered modernities: Ethnographic perspectives.* New York: Palgrave Macmillan

Homewood N (2018) The fantastic fetus: The fetus as a super-citizen in Ghanaian Pentecostalism. *Citizenship Studies* 22(6): 618–632

hooks b (2000) *Feminism is for everybody: Passionate politics.* Cambridge, MA: South End Press

Horn J (2006) Re-righting the sexual body. *Feminist Africa* 6: 7–19

Hungwe C (2006) Putting them in their place: 'Respectable' and 'unrespectable' women in Zimbabwean gender struggles. *Feminist Africa 6: Subaltern Sexualities*: 33–47

Hunt S (1995) A new marketplace: The growing new religious movements of Eastern Europe. *Frontier* June–August: 8–11

Hunt S (2000) 'Winning ways': Globalisation and the impact of the health and wealth gospel. *Journal of Contemporary Religion* 15(3): 331–347

Isichei CR (2004) *The religious traditions of Africa: A history.* Westport, CT: Praeger Publishers

Jacobs-Huey L (2002) The natives are gazing and talking back: Reviewing the problematics of positionality, voice, and accountability among 'native' anthropologists. *American Anthropologist* 104(3): 791–804

James D (2019) New subjectivities: Aspiration, prosperity and the new middle class. *African Studies* 78(1): 33–50

Johnson EA (1984) The incomprehensibility of God and the image of God male and female. *Theological Studies* 45(3): 441–465

Jones SH, Adams TE & Ellis C (Eds) (2016). *Handbook of autoethnography.* New York: Routledge

Jordaan R (1987) The emergence of Black feminist theology in South Africa. *Journal of Black Theology in South Africa* 1(2): 42–46

Kalu OU (2010) The big man of the big God: Popular culture, media and African Pentecostal missionary strategy. In WK Kalu, N Wariboko & T Falola (Eds) *Christian missions in Africa: Success, ferment and trauma* (Vol. 2). Asmara: African World Press

KaNdlondlo M (2011) When sacrificing self is the only way out: A tribute to my mother. *Agenda* 25(1): 15–21

Khanyile S (2016) The virtualization of the church: New media representations of neo-Pentecostal performance(s) in South Africa. MA thesis, University of the Witwatersrand

Khanyile S (2017) Extreme and the exceptional: A multimodal critical discourse analysis of social media representations of neo-Pentecostals in South African journalism. *Comunicare* 12(4): 48–66

Kirsch TG (2015) The Universal Church of the Kingdom of God in South Africa: A church of strangers. *Anthropology Southern Africa* 38(3–4): 378–380

Koegelenberg R (2012) *Men in the pulpit, women in the pew? Addressing gender inequality in Africa.* Stellenbosch: Sun Press

Kolapo FJ (2019) Nigeria's Pentecostal churches and the tribunal of social media. *Social Media* 26: 1–18

Kroesbergen H (Ed.) (2014) *In search of health and wealth: The prosperity gospel in African, reformed perspective.* Oregon: Wipf & Stock

Kuponu SI (2015) Pentecostalism and media: A reflection on space contestation on the internet. *International Journal of Social Sciences and Humanities Reviews* 5(1): 70–74

Landman C (1995) Ten years of feminist theology in South Africa. *Journal of Feminist Studies in Religion* 11(1): 143–148

Lane N (2016) Bringing flesh to theory: Ethnography, Black queer theory, and studying Black sexualities. *Feminist Studies* 42(3): 632–648

Laurent PJ (2001) Transnationalisation and local transformations: The example of the Church of Assemblies of God of Burkina Faso. In A Corten & RR Marshall-Fratani (Eds) *Between Babel and Pentecost: Transnational Pentecostalism in Africa and Latin America*. Bloomington: Indiana University Press

Lindhardt M (2015) Men of God: Neo-Pentecostalism and masculinities in urban Tanzania. *Religion* 45(2): 252–272

Lorde A (2007) *Sister outsider: Essays and speeches*. New York: Ten Speed Press

Lutwama-Rukundo E (2016) Skimpy fashion and sexuality in Sheebah Karungi's performances. *Feminist Africa* 21: 52–62

Maluleke T & Nadar S (2002) Breaking the covenant of violence against women. *Journal of Theology for Southern Africa* 5(114): 5–17

Mama A (1995) *Beyond the masks: Race, gender and subjectivity*. New York: Routledge

Mapuranga TP (2013) Bargaining with patriarchy? Women Pentecostal leaders in Zimbabwe. *Fieldwork in Religion* 8(1): 74–91

Mapuranga TP (2018) Pastors, preachers and wives: A critical reflection on the role of Pentecostalism in women empowerment in Zimbabwe. In L Togarasei (Ed.) *Aspects of Pentecostal Christianity in Zimbabwe*. New York: Springer

Marshall-Fratani R (1998) Mediating the global and the local in Nigerian Pentecostalism. *Journal of Religion in Africa* 28(3): 278–315

Martin B (2003) The Pentecostal gender paradox: A cautionary tale for the sociology of religion. In RK Fenn (Ed.) *The Blackwell companion to sociology of religion*. Oxford: Blackwell

Masenya J (1994) A feminist perspective on theology with particular reference to Black feminist theology. *Scriptura: Journal for Biblical, Theological and Contextual Hermeneutics* 49: 64–74

Masenya M (1995) African womanist hermeneutics: A suppressed voice from South Africa speaks. *Journal of Feminist Studies in Religion* 11(1): 149–155.

Masenya M (1997b) Redefining ourselves: A bosadi (womanhood) approach. *Old Testament Essays* 10(3): 439–448

Masenya M (1999) Biblical authority and the authority of women's experiences: Whither way? *Scriptura: Journal for Biblical, Theological and Contextual Hermeneutics* 70: 229–240

Masenya M (2005) An African methodology for South African biblical sciences: Revisiting the bosadi (womanhood) approach. *Old Testament Essays* 18(3): 741–751

Mate R (2002) Wombs as God's laboratories: Pentecostal discourses of femininity in Zimbabwe. *Africa* 72(4): 549–568

Matuku S & Kaseke E (2014) The role of stokvels in improving people's lives: The case in Orange Farm, Johannesburg, South Africa. *Social Work* 50(4): 504–515

Mayekiso M (1996) *Township politics: Civic struggles for a new South Africa.* New York: Monthly Review Press

Mbewe C (2011) A letter from Kabwata. Accessed 23 October 2019, http://www. conradmbewe.com/2011/02/nigerian-religious-junk.html

McCauley JF (2012) Africa's new big man rule? Pentecostalism and patronage in Ghana. *African Affairs* 112(446): 1–21

McClaurin I (2001) Forging a theory, politics, praxis, and poetics of black feminist anthropology. In I McClaurin (Ed.) *Black feminist anthropology: Theory, politics, praxis, and poetics.* New Brunswick, NJ: Rutgers University Press

McCutcheon RT (Ed.) (1999) *The insider/outsider problem in the study of religion: A reader.* London: Continuum

McElhinny B (2003) Theorising gender in sociolinguistic and linguistic anthropology. In J Holmes & M Meyerhoff (Eds) *The handbook of language and gender.* Oxford: Blackwell

Meyer B (1998) 'Make a complete break with the past': Memory and post-colonial modernity in Ghanaian Pentecostalist discourse. *Journal of Religion in Africa* 27(3): 316–349

Meyer B (1999) *Translating the devil: Religion and modernity among the Ewe in Ghana.* Edinburgh: Edinburgh University Press

Meyer B (2004) Christianity in Africa: From African independent to Pentecostal-Charismatic Churches. *Annual Review of Anthropology* 33: 447–474

Meyer B (2006) Impossible representations: Pentecostalism, vision and video technology in Ghana. In B Meyer & A Moors (Eds) *Religion, media and the public sphere.* Bloomington: Indiana University Press

Meyer B (2007) Pentecostalism and neo-liberal capitalism: Faith, prosperity and vision in African Pentecostal-Charismatic churches. *Journal for the Study of Religion* 20(2): 5–28

Mhongo C (2013) Declining rates of marriage in South Africa: What do the numbers and analysts say? *Acta Juridica* 1: 181–196

Miller D & Yamamori T (2007) *Global Pentecostalism: The new face of Christian social engagement.* Berkeley: University of California Press

Milner IV HR (2007) Race, culture, and researcher positionality: Working through dangers seen, unseen, and unforeseen. *Educational Researcher* 36(7): 388–400

Moraga, C. and Anzaldúa, G. eds., 2022. *This bridge called my back: Writings by radical women of color.* New York: State University of New York Press

Motsemme N (2004a) The mute always speak: On women's silences at the Truth and Reconciliation Commission. *Current Sociology* 52(5): 909–932

Motsemme N (2004b) The meanings in silence: Memory. *Rhodes Journalism Review* 24: 4–5

Mose Brown T & De Casanova EM (2014) Representing the language of the 'other': African American vernacular English in ethnography. *Ethnography* 15(2): 208–231

Moya PM (1997) Postmodernism, 'realism', and the politics of identity: Cherrie Moraga and Chicana feminism. In MJ Alexander & CT Mohanty (Eds) *Feminist genealogies, colonial legacies, democratic futures.* New York: Routledge

Mupotsa D (2011) From nation to family: Researching gender and sexuality. In C Cramer, L Hammond & J Pottier (Eds), *Researching violence in Africa: Ethical and methodological challenges.* Leiden: Brill

Mupotsa D (2014) White weddings. PhD thesis, University of the Witwatersrand

Mupotsa D (2015a) Becoming girl-woman-bride. *Girlhood Studies* 8(3): 73–87

Mupotsa D (2015b) The promise of happiness: Desire, attachment and freedom in post/apartheid South Africa. *Critical Arts* 29(2): 183–198

Mupotsa DS (2020) Conjugality. *GLQ: A Journal of Lesbian and Gay Studies* 26(3): 377–403

Musangi NS (2018) Homing with my mother / how women in my family married women. *Meridians* 17(2): 401–414

Mwaura P & Parsitau D (2012) Perceptions of women's health and rights in Christian new religious movements in Kenya. In A Adogame, E Chitando & B Bateye (Eds) *African traditions in the study of religions in Africa.* Farnham: Ashgate

Nadar S (2005a) On being Pentecostal church: Pentecostal women's voices and visions. In IA Phiri & S Nadar (Eds) *On being church: African women's voices and visions.* Geneva: World Council of Churches

Nadar S (2005b) Searching the dungeons beneath our religious discourses: The case of violence against women and the 'unholy trinity'. *Agenda*, 19(66): 16–22

Nadar S (2009a) Changing the world: The task of feminist biblical scholars. *Journal of Feminist Studies in Religion* 55(2): 137–143

Nadar S (2009b) Palatable patriarchy and violence against wo/men in South Africa: Angus Buchan's Mighty Men's Conference as a case study of masculinism. *Scriptura: Journal for Contextual Hermeneutics in Southern Africa* 102(1): 551–561

Nadar S (2019) 'Stories are data with soul': Lessons from black feminist epistemology. In T Oren & AL Press (Eds) *The Routledge handbook of contemporary feminism.* New York: Routledge

Nadar S & Potgieter C (2010) *Liberated through submission?* The Worthy Woman's Conference as a case study of formenism. *Journal of Feminist Studies in Religion* 26(2): 141–151

Newell S (2007) Pentecostal witchcraft: Neoliberal possession and demonic discourse in Ivoirian Pentecostal churches. *Journal of Religion in Africa* 37: 461–490

Ngcobo L & Chisasa J (2018) Success factors and gender participation of stokvels in South Africa. *Acta Universitatis Danubius Economica* 14(5): 217–228

Nortjé-Meyer L (2011) A critical analysis of Gretha Wiid's sex ideology and her biblical hermeneutics. *Verbum et Ecclesia* 32(1): 1–7

Ogunyemi CO (1985) Womanism: The dynamics of the contemporary black female novel in English. *Signs: Journal of Women in Culture and Society* 11(1): 63–80

O'Hara KP, Massimi M, Harper R, Rubens S & Morris J (2014) Everyday dwelling with WhatsApp. *Proceedings of the 17th ACM conference on computer supported cooperative work & social computing.* New York: ACM Press

Oraegbunam IK (2006) From patriarchy to women empowerment: Socio-religious challenges and prospects. *Gender and Behaviour* 4(2): 852–866

Owens L, Edwards EB & McArthur SA (2018) Black women researchers' path to breaking silence: Three scholars reflect on voicing oppression, self-reflexive speech, and talking back to elite discourses. *Western Journal of Black Studies* 42(3–4): 125–135

Parsitau DS (2009) 'Keep holy distance and abstain till He comes': Interrogating a Pentecostal church's engagements with HIV/AIDS and the youth in Kenya. *Africa Today* 56(1): 44–64

Parsitau DS (2020) Women without limits and limited women: Pentecostal women navigating between empowerment and disempowerment in Kenya. In FB Nyamnjoh & JA Carpenter (Eds) *Christianity and social change in contemporary Africa: Volume one.* Bamenda: Langaa RPCIG

Parsitau DS & Mwaura PN (2010) God in the city: Pentecostalism as an urban phenomenon in Kenya. *Studia Historiae Ecclesiasticae* 36(2): 95–112

Patterson A & Kuperus T (2016) Mobilizing the faithful: Organizational autonomy, visionary pastors, and citizenship in South Africa and Zambia. *African Affairs* 115(459): 318–341

Pearce TO (2012) Reconstructing sexuality in the shadow of neoliberal globalization: Investigating the approach of Charismatic churches in southwestern Nigeria. *Journal of Religion in Africa* 42: 345–368

Pierce Y (2013) Womanist ways and Pentecostalism: The work of recovery and critique. *Pneuma* 35(1): 24–34

Phillips L (Ed.) (2006) *The womanist reader.* New York: Routledge

Phillips L & McCaskill B (2006) Who's schooling who? Black women and the bringing of the everyday into academe, or why we started *The Womanist* (1995). In L Phillips (Ed.) *The womanist reader.* New York: Routledge

Phiri IA (2004) A theological analysis of the voices of teenage girls on 'men's role in the fight against HIV/AIDS' in KwaZulu-Natal, South Africa. *Journal of Theology for Southern Africa* 120: 34–45

Posel D, Rudwick S & Casale D (2011) Is marriage a dying institution in South Africa? Exploring changes in marriage in context of *ilobolo* payments. *Agenda* 25(1): 102–111

Premawardhana D (2015) Ilana van Wyk, the Universal Church of the Kingdom of God in South Africa: A church of strangers. *Africa* 85(4): 729–730

Prinsloo J (2018) (Con)textual gymnastics: Critical discourse analysis. In KG Tomaselli (Ed.) *Making sense of research.* Pretoria: Van Schaik

Pype K (2009) Media celebrity, charisma and morality in post-Mobutu Kinshasa. *Journal of Southern African Studies* 35(3): 541–555

Pype K (2012) *The making of the Pentecostal melodrama: Religion, media and gender in Kinshasa.* New York: Berghahn Books

Quayesi-Amakye J (2011) Prosperity and prophecy in African Pentecostalism. *Journal of Pentecostal Theology* 20: 291–305

Quiroz S (2016) The dilemmas of monogamy: Pleasure, discipline and the Pentecostal moral self in the Republic of Benin. *Religions* 102(7): 1–16

Ramphele M (2000) Teach me how to be a man: An exploration of the definition of masculinity. In V Das, A Kleinman, M Ramphele & P Reynolds (Eds) *Violence and subjectivity.* Berkeley: University of California Press

Richardson, JE (2007) *Analysing newspapers: An approach from critical discourse analysis.* New York: Palgrave Macmillan

Roberts C (1997) The politics of transcription. *TESOL Quarterly* 31(1): 167–172

Rodriguez C (2001) A homegirl goes home: Black feminism and the lure of native anthropology. In I McClaurin (Ed.) *Black feminist anthropology: Theory, politics, praxis and poetics*. New Brunswick, NJ: Rutgers University Press

Rubin G (1984) Thinking sex: Notes for a radical theory on the politics of sexuality. In C Vance (Ed.) *Pleasure and danger: Exploring female sexuality*. London: Routledge & Kegan Paul

Rudwick S & Posel D (2013) Changing patterns of marriage and cohabitation in South Africa. *Acta Juridica* 1: 169–180

Sackey BM (2006) *New directions in gender and religion: The changing status of women in African independent churches*. Lanham: Lexington Books

Sande N (2019) The Pentecostal theology and gender-based violence. *International Journal of Contemporary Applied Researches* 6(2): 1–12

Schenectady GD & Parsitau D (2017) Empowered to submit: Pentecostal women in Nairobi. *Journal of Religion & Society* 19: 1–18

Shooter S (2014) How feminine participation in the divine might renew the church and its leadership. *Feminist Theology* 22(2): 173–185

Sjørup L (2002) Pentecostals: The power of the powerless. *Dialog: A Journal of Theology* 41(1): 16–25

Soothill J (2007) *Gender, social change and spiritual power: Charismatic Christianity in Ghana*. Leiden: Brill

Soothill J (2019) A critical approach to concepts of 'power' and 'agency' in Ghana's Charismatic (or neo-Pentecostal) churches. In J Casselberry & EA Pritchard (Eds) *Spirit on the move: Black women and Pentecostalism in Africa and the diaspora*. Durham, NC: Duke University Press

Sperber E & Hern E (2018) Pentecostal identity and citizen engagement in sub-Saharan Africa: New evidence from Zambia. *Politics and Religion* 11: 830–862

Spillers HJ (1987) Mamas baby, papas maybe: An American grammar book. *Diacritics* 17(2): 64–81

Spivak GC (1988) Can the subaltern speak? In C Nelson & L Grossberg (Eds) *Marxism and the interpretation of culture*. Basingstoke: Macmillan

Stoll D (1990) *Is Latin America turning Protestant? The politics of evangelical growth*. Berkeley: University of California Press

Tamale S (2011) Researching and theorising sexualities in Africa. In S Tamale (Ed.) *African sexualities*. Cape Town: Pambazuka Press

Tamale S (2014) Exploring the contours of African sexualities: Religion, law and power. *African Human Rights Law Journal* 14(1): 150–177

Tamale S (2016) 'Keep your eyes off my thighs': A feminist analysis of Uganda's 'miniskirt law'. *Feminist Africa* 21: 83–90

Tannen D, Hamilton HE & Schiffrin D (Eds) (2015) T*he handbook of discourse analysis* (2nd ed.). Chichester: John Wiley & Sons

Togarasei L (2005) Modern Pentecostalism as an urban phenomenon: The case of the Family of God Church in Zimbabwe. *Exchange* 34(4): 349–376

Togarasei L (2011) The Pentecostal gospel of prosperity in African contexts of poverty: An appraisal. *Exchange* 40: 336–350

Togarasei L (2012) Mediating the Gospel: Pentecostal Christianity and media technology in Botswana and Zimbabwe. *Journal of Contemporary Religion* 27(2): 257–274

Togarasei L (2015) Modern/Charismatic Pentecostalism as a form of 'religious' secularisation in Africa. *Studia Historiae Ecclesiasticae* 41(1): 56–66

Trouillot MR (2003) *Global transformations*: Anthropology and the modern world. New York: Palgrave Macmillan

Tuckey C & Kretzschmar L (2002) Socialisation, sexism, children and the church. *Missionalia* 30(3): 389–409

Van de Kamp L (2016) The Universal Church of the Kingdom of God in South Africa: A church of strangers. *Religion and Society* 7: 164–166

Van Dijk R (1992) *Young Malawian puritans: Young puritan preachers in a present-day African urban environment*. Utrecht: ISOR

Van Dijk R (1998) Fundamentalism, cultural memory and the state: Contested representations of time in postcolonial Malawi. In R Werbner (Ed.) *In memory and the postcolony: African anthropology and the critique of power*. London: Zed Books

Van Dijk R (2013) Counselling and Pentecostal modalities of social engineering of relationships in Botswana. *Culture, Health & Sexuality* 15(4): 509–522

Van Dijk TA (1993) Principles of critical discourse analysis. *Discourse and Society* 4(2): 249–283

Van Klinken A (2011) Male headship as male agency: An alternative understanding of a 'patriarchal' African Pentecostal discourse on masculinity. *Religion and Gender* 1(1): 104–124

Van Klinken A (2012) Men in the remaking: Conversion narratives and born-again masculinity in Zambia. *Journal of Religion in Africa* 42(3): 215–239

Van Klinken A (2016) Pentecostalism, political masculinity and citizenship. *Journal of Religion in Africa* 46: 129–157

Van Klinken A & Obadare E (2018) Christianity, sexuality and citizenship in Africa: Critical intersections. *Citizenship Studies* 22(6): 557–568

Van Wyk I (2014) *The Universal Church of the Kingdom of God in South Africa: A church of strangers*. New York: Cambridge University Press

Vels N (2013) Want to be in my gang? Power, prestige, possession and the search for Christian identity in South Africa. *Journal of Theology for Southern Africa* 146: 122–138

Verhoef G (2001) Informal financial service institutions for survival: African women and stokvels in urban South Africa, 1930–1988. *Enterprise & Society* 2(2): 259–296

Verrips J (2002) Screens and our corporeal eye. *Etnofoor* 15(1–2): 21–46

Walker A (1983) *In search of our mothers' gardens: Womanist prose*. San Diego: Harcourt Brace Jovanovich

Weems RJ (1991) Reading her way through the struggle. In CH Felder (Ed.) *The Bible and liberation: Political and social liberation*. Minneapolis, MN: Fortress Press

Whitehead AL (2012) Gender ideology and religion: Does a masculine image of God matter? *Review of Religious Research* 54(2): 139–156

Williams DS (2006) Womanist theology: Black women's voices. In L Phillips (Ed.) *The womanist reader*. New York: Routledge

Zinn MC (1979) Field research in minority communities: Ethical, methodological and political observations by an insider. *Social Problems* 27(2): 209–219

Index

A

abazalwane xi
adoption 25
adultery 33, 34
African
    feminism 8, 12, 45, 50
    gender discourses 32–39
    Pentecostalism, scholarship on
        12–14, 17
    sexuality 34–35
    traditions, and modernity 15–17
    women, representations of 20–21,
        57
agency xi-xii, 9, 15, 24, 26, 36, 39,
        42-43, 75-76, 89, 106-7
Alexandra 10, 62, 64, *124*, *125*
Americanised megachurches 46
apartheid 3, 10, 23, 36, 61
Apostolic Faith Mission 3
argumentation, use of 58
Assemblies of God 3

B

bazalwane 66, 67, 68, 78, 127n13
beauty
    ideas of 72
    and moralistic codes 35, 36
Bethesda 3
biblical texts, interpretation/s of 7,
        30–31, 90, 99
Bishop Silawuli 2, *120*
    approach to femininity of 83
    on equality of the sexes 81
    interaction with 48–49
    wedding ceremony by 74–76
Black
    feminism 7–8
    feminist theology 6–7, 12
    liberation movements 6
    middleclass 15, 16,
Black women
    and Black feminism 7–8
    and Black feminist theology 6–7
    and Blackwomen scholarship 8,
        9, 32, 59
    and the Bosadi approach 6–7

constructed identity of 30–31
and gendered discourses 5
and marriage 86
and sexuality 34, 35, 36, 44
and slavery 37
and whiteness 40, 57
Blackwomen
    researchers 32, 44, 59
    scholarship xiii, 8, 9
    theory xiii, 8, 9, 44, 48
blessing-theology 4
body language 53
body-styling choices 102
boMshoza 30, 126n8
born again (Christians) xi, 9, 15, 19,
        24, 66, 91, 103
Bosadi (Womanhood) theology 6–7
Botswana 7, 23, 25
bride 40, 42, 47, 73-75, 77

C

capitalism 8, 13, 15, 16, 33
careers for women, and the
        patriarchal system 22
celibacy
    and the dating process 105
    freedom from 75
Charismatic moral codes 19–20
Charismatic Pentecostalism
    attractiveness for women of 4–5
    in South Africa 3
Charismatics 3, 13, 15, 19
child abuse 77
childbearing 34, 82, 83, 116, 118
childhood memories 61
childlessness 25
children
    and economic male power 33
    and marriage 82, 83, 91, 104, 110
Christian motherhood 22
    see also motherhood
Christianity
    in Africa 3
    and inferior identity for African
        women 30–31
    and laws and politics 32, 33, 34

markers of proper 115, 116, 117
and political identities 4
church
    congregation/service 51–52, 63, 64–65, 66, 67–68
    venues 61, 62–63, 64, 65, 66, 67
    wedding 73–77
cis-gender women 113
clapping 62, 63, 64, 67
colonial 35, 37, 38, 44
colonisation
    of femininity 72, 93–94
    gendered 36
    of the subaltern 43
Comaroff, Jean and John 12–13
commercialism, and religion 18, 19
communal churches 46
congregation/service
    at God's Love 65–66, 69–70
    at Living Waters 62–63, 64, 68, 84
    at Red Sea 66–67, 70–71, 73, 84
    at Upper Hall 64–65, 69, 71, 83, 84
    see also sermons
conservative religious discourse, on sexuality 34
courting 107, 109, 127n25
critical discourse analysis 57–58

D
dancing 25, 66, 67, 98, 99
data
    collected 53, 54, 56
    translation of 56, 57
democracy, South Africa's transition to 3, 4
Democratic Republic of the Congo 13
difference
    anthropologists' approaches to 115
    and freedom 117–118
    and spirithood 116, 117, 118
    ways of handling 115
Dillard, Cynthia B. 47
domestic
    power 33
    violence 21
dress codes/rules
    and church 68, 69, 70, 84, 94, 116
    and moralistic codes 35–36

and participants' responses/views 94–98, 100, 102–104, 112, 113, 116

E
economic power, of men 33
embodiment
    possibilities of 87
    of religious community by Black women 31, 32, 40
emotion 77, 78, 113
    cultural politics of 43
empowerment of women 7, 23, 36, 39, 79, 80, 99, 102
engagement (to be married) 73, 75, 77
entertainment domain, and Pentecostalism 19–20
entrepreneurship 15
epistemology 6, 7, 43, 47, 57, 93
equality
    the term 50/50 and 81, 88–90
    definitions of 88–94
    in Pentecostal spaces 26
    of the sexes 81
ethical considerations 59
ethics 20, 27, 33, 51
ethnographic methodology 54, 56, 57, 59
ethnography 46, 47, 48, 56, 58, 59
evangelical movements, and sexuality 34
evangelising 127n16
evangelisation, and social media 20

F
fashion, and moral/moralistic codes 36
fear factory 37, 94–102
female
    fear factory 94–102
    leadership, in Pentecostal churches 21, 26, 27, 92
    subordination 23, 31, 90, 91
femicide 77
feminine
    absurdity 42, 43
    identities 5, 31
femininity
    and difference 115, 116
    construction of 58

cult of 36, 80, 101
definitions of 35
and gendered identity 11
and heteronormativity 87
and ideas of beauty 72
in patriarchal terms 83
and power networks 31
and respectability 35, 41, 72, 83, 116
spiritual 116
varying constructions of 112
and 'white weddings' 40, 41
feminist
epistemology 47
ethnography 56, 57, 58, 59
liberation 6
scholarship 46, 47, 48
theology 6–7, 12
field notes 53
flesh 8–9, 37–39, 42, 48
for*men*ism 22, 23, 26, 88

G
gender(ed)
construction 99, 101
differences 73, 113
discourses 44, 58
discrimination 6
equality 26, 81, 88–94
and heterosexuality 41, 87
identities 5, 9, 11, 21–27, 31, 40, 41, 71, 85
ideologies 21–27, 58, 71, 90
instability of 42
as performativity 40–41
non-conformity 102
relations, transformation in 24–25
and sexuality 35, 96, 101
and shame 96, 97, 98, 100, 109, 116
values 5
gender-based violence 36–37, 38, 77, 101–102
Ghana 18, 19, 25, 26, 92
God, nature of 78–79
God's Love Ministries 2, 21, 52, *60*, 65, 67, 69–70, 84, 97, 99, *120*
Gomora 10, 126n3
see also Alexandra
gospel music 17

Gqola, Pumla Dineo 7–8, 36, 37, 101–102
Grace Bible Church 15, 16, 17, 74

H
happiness 71, 73, 76
and heterosexuality 85–88, 114, 116
and whiteness xii, xiii
health and wealth ministries 14
heteronormativity xiii, 82, 85, 87, 113, 116
heterosexism 117
heterosexuality
and domesticity 34, 83
and femininity 40, 41
and happiness 85, 86, 87, 88, 116
and marriage 84–87
and possibilities of embodiment 87
His People Church 15, 16
Holy Spirit, and liberation 99, 102, 104
homophobic system 36
homosexuality, law against 34
hooks, bell 118

I
inequality 14, 15, 71
inferiority, and feminine identity 22, 31, 88
insider/outsider space (of researcher) 47, 56
intergenerational relationships 49, 50
internet 18
interview technique 54, 55
Islam 32, 33, 34
Ivory Coast 16

K
Kenya 13, 15, 25
kitchen tea parties 51
Ko Bareng 64, *122, 123*

L
land rights 10
language
of the church 56
note on vii
of prayer 67–68
of quotations 56–57, 59

silence as 43, 93
LGBTQI+ movements 25, 126n6
liberation
    hermeneutics 6, 79
    and the Holy Spirit 99, 102, 104
Living Waters Ministries 2, 51–52,
        62, 64, 67, 68, 84, 94, 95, 102
lobola 16, 74–75, 76
Lorde, Audre 11, 77, 115, 118

M
male
    children 33
    dominance 77, 81, 82
    God 112
    gods xiii
    leadership 24
    moralists 35
    responsibilisation 24
    superiority 88
male headship
    women's views on 88–94, 107,
        112, 113
    and the 'Word of God' 89, 90
marriage
    agreement of 75
    and childlessness 25
    desire for 85, 86, 113, 116
    and mediators 75
    rites 45
    role of men in 76–77
masculinity
    defining of 23
    discourses on 24
    toxic 77
    see also Pentecostal masculinity
Masenya, Madipoane 6–7, 12
media, Charismatic churches' use of
        13, 14, 17, 18, 19
    see also social media
mediatisation of religion in Africa
        18–21, 29
megachurches 9, 13, 15, 16, 17, 20,
        27, 29, 46
Messianic religious texts 32, 33
Methodist Church 61, 66
middleclass 4, 15
Mighty Men's Conference (MMC) 23
miniskirt law 35, 96, 97
miracle healing 21
miracle-focused pastors 13

modernity, Pentecostal movement
        and 4, 15, 16, 17, 18, 93
monogamy 33
moral
    capitalism 16
    codes 19, 35–36, 96, 98
    teachings 93–94
moralistic
    discourses on sexuality 34, 35, 36
    demands and Christianity 38–39
    rules of sexuality 95–96
motherhood 22, 26, 72, 105, 109, 114
Mupotsa, Danai 32, 40, 41, 42, 44, 54
music 17, 64, 81

N
Nadar, Sorojini 22, 23, 38–39, 47, 88,
        90, 99, 102
narrative analysis 11, 58–59
'narrative knowing' 7
New Pentecostals 3
Ngqula, Umvangeli (Evangelist) 65
Nigeria 19, 20, 34
Nomfalweni, Fuzeka see Pastor
        Fuzeka
nuclear family 16,
Nyathi, Petrus see Pastor Nyathi
Nyathi, Rose (Pastor) 2, 51, 62, 63, 68

O
oppression
    and construction of difference
        117
    and counterstrategies 39
    and discursive strategies 71
    and domains/modes of power 80
    forms of 6
    internalised 117, 118
    and patriarchy 8, 21–22
    view on xii
ordainment of women 2, 26, 27, 69,
        83

P
participants (research)
    on the dating process 105–108
    on equality and gender roles
        88– 94
    finding of 50–51, 52
    and interview technique 54–56,
        58, 59

on love and marriage 85–86, 113
and male headship 88, 89, 90, 91,
    107, 113
and parents and family 108–109,
    114
and respectability 92, 95–97,
    102–104, 109, 113–114, 116
and rules of sexuality 94–105
on sexism 104–105
and sisterhood 111–112, 114
and spiritual mothers/fathers
    109–110
pass laws 10
Pastor
    Fuzeka 2, 65–66, 69, 78, 79, 84,
        112
    Mabaso 71, 82
    Nyathi 2, 62, 63, 81, 82, 83, 112
    Patrick 21, 69, 70, *120*
    Silawuli 48, 50, 63, 64
    Thoko (author's mother) 48, 49,
        50, 55, *60*, *120*
    Xoli (anonymised name) 2, 76–77,
        78, 79, 113
pastoralisation 23
patriarchal
    bargaining 23, 90
    capitalism 33
    context/interpretation of the Bible
        90, 99
    ideology 21–22, 81, 88
    imagery of God 31
    practices and spirituality 39, 99
    structures 21, 36, 59, 80, 88
    system 36
    terms, and construction of
        femininity 83
patriarchy
    critique of 89
    and difference 116, 117
    and feminism 7–8, 43
    and for*men*ism 23
    and gendered ideas 21, 22
    and respectability 35, 97
    and silent resistance 93, 94
patronage system 14
Pentecostal
    history 3–5
    femininity, paradox of 5, 11, 32,
        42, 43, 44, 89, 92, 113
    masculinity 24, 77

movement, and modernity 15
research, representations of
    African women in 57
studies, anthropological approach
    to xiii
Pentecostal churches
    in Africa 3, 4
    in Alexandra 2, 111
    history of 3
    and political involvement 16
    and prosperity 14
    and sexual education 25
    and social media 20
    in sub-Saharan Africa 25
    in Uganda 19–20
    white 4
Pentecostalism
    conversion to 61, 127n22
    independent branches of 3
    and political identities 4
    systems of power within 21
performativity, gender as 40–41
Phutaditjaba Community Centre *122*
plurality (of sexualities) 25, 35
political
    identities 4
    involvement, and Pentecostal
        churches 16–17
    power 36
    religions 33
politics, of the 1980s 3
pop culture 17, 22
positionality (of researchers) of 13,
    14, 29, 45, 47
postmodernity 32
power networks, women's resistance
    to 31
praise songs 67, 74
prayer
    camps 25–26
    scarves (*doeks*) 94–96
promiscuity 24
prophetization 23
prosperity gospel 9, 13, 14, 15, 17,
    20, 46
psychologisation 23

R
racial discrimination 6, 10
racism xiii, 8, 117

Red Sea Ministries 2, 52, 53, *60*, 66,
70–71, 73, 84
religion, and commercialism 18, 19
research methodology 10, 59
research participants *see* participants
respectability
codes of 118
and domesticity 34, 83
and dress code 35, 69, 94, 96,
103–104, 113, 116
and female fear factory 94–102
and femininity 35, 41, 72, 83, 116
and heterosexuality 41, 83
laws of 35
of marriage 82
and masculinity 24
participants view of 92, 95–97,
102–104, 109, 113–114, 116
and sexuality 72
responsibility
and Blackwomen researchers/
scholarship 8, 9, 32, 59
and masculinity 24, 77
of women and dress codes 100,
101
return soldier 104, 127n24
Rhema 3
rhetorical practice 58
rights of women 34, 35
Rustenburg Declaration' (1990) 3

S
sati suicide 42
scarves (*doeks*), wearing of 68,
94–96, 103, 113
secularisation 17
sermons
analysis of 2, 11, 16, 57–58, 88
and aspects of femininity 58
and constructions of femininity
105, 112, 113, 115–116
and gender identities 71, 72, 73,
76–77
by men 81–83
and patriarchal ideology/
structures 81–82, 88–90
recording of 48, 53, 56
style of 67–68
transcription of 56
by women 78–80
see also congregation

service *see* congregation; sermons
servitude, and patriarchal structures
22, 88–89, 90
sexism 104, 105, 113, 117
sexual education
and counselling 25
and 'ex-gay men' 25
and self-control 24, 25,
sexual orientation 33, 102
sexuality
conservative religious discourse
on 33, 34
description of 33, 72
and domesticity 34, 83
and enslavement 37
and the 'fear factory' 37
and gender 35, 96, 101
and laws of respectability 35, 36
and legislation 33, 34
and moralistic codes 36
and 'political religions' 33
and shame 98
and spirituality 95, 96, 98–99
and whiteness 40
see also heterosexuality
Shabangu, Xolile (anonymised name)
see Pastor Xoli
shaming (of women)
and dress codes 96, 97, 98, 102
and feminine obligations 97, 100,
109, 116
Silawuli, Luvuyo *see* Bishop Silawuli
Silawuli, Nkuli 3, *11*, 50–51, 64, 69,
121
silence
and abuse 36, 101, 111
as negotiation 91, 93
in resistance 43, 58
silenced 36, 58, 87
singing 25, *60*, 63, 64–65, 66, 67
single motherhood 105, 109, 114,
Sixoka, Patrick *see* Pastor Patrick
slavery, and gender-based violence 37
social media
and evangelisation 20
uses by churches of 16, 20–21
socioeconomic development 14
soft patriarchy 81, 88, 112
South Africa
Black feminist theology in 6–7
Pentecostal history in 3–4

and transition to democracy
23–24
spiritual femininity 116
spirituality
interpretation/s of 7
patriarchal 39, 99
and sexuality 95, 96, 98–99
Spivak, Gayatri Chakravorty 42, 43,
93
stereotypes 35, 41
stokvels 62
street vendors 62
subjugation of the feminine 9, 31
submission
to authorities 25
and domestic violence 21
to a husband 22, 23
public persona of 92
views on 88
and wilfulness 11
subordination, female 23, 31, 90, 91
substance abuse 24
suicide 42, 43, 93
superstition 27

T
Tanzania 24, 92
tithing 14, 15, 28, 48, 63
transcription 56, 57
translation viii, 56, 57
Twala, Linda 66

U
Uganda 19–20, 34, 35, 36, 96, 97
Ugandan 'miniskirt law' 35, 96, 97
unethical scholarship 27, 29
'unholy trinity' 38–39, 99–100, 101,
102
Universal Church of the Kingdom of
God 27–28
Upper Hall Ministries 2, 50, 51, 63,
64, 69, 71, 83, 84, 85–87
upward mobility 14, 16, 17, 84

V
Van Wyk, Ilana 27–28
violence

and gendered ideologies 21, 25
and patriarchal structures 36
and sexuality 33, 34, 35, 37
see also gender-based violence
volunteers *see* participants

W
Weberian theory 26
websites, of Pentecostal churches
20–21
wedding
and African traditions 75–76
announcement 71, 73
ceremony 74–76
discourse 87
rituals 40, 47
see also white weddings
Western
feminist theories 6
thought 35
traditions 15
WhatsApp, use of 52, 53
white weddings' 32, 40, 41, 47
whiteness
and Black women 57
and happiness xii, xiii
and sexuality 40
witchcraft 15, 28
womanism 8
womanist
hermeneutics 7
theology 6–7
women
ordainment of 2, 26, 27, 69, 83
and submission 11, 21, 22, 23, 25,
88, 92
women's rights
and biblical interpretations 30–31
and sexuality 34, 35
worship leaders 3, *11*, 67
Worthy Women's Conference 22, 23

Z
Zion Christian Church 21, 62
Zionist movement 3
Zozo huts 66, 127n14